NIKKI GOLDSTEIN

GirlForce *friends*

A girl's guide to friendship

ABC
Books

Contents

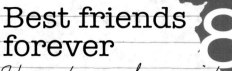
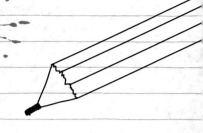

Hi Everyone

Over the past few years I've been running a weekly on-line forum, that has attracted hundreds of girls from all over Australia. We use the opportunity to talk about everything from boys to zits, parents to time management and school studies. But by far the biggest topic of the forum has been friendship. Each week girls log on with requests for support and advice about how to manage buddies, bullies, BFs and friendship meltdowns. The overwhelming demand for advice on this subject prompted me to call my friend Sarah Oakes, the former editor of *Girlfriend* magazine and ask if we could do another big survey through the magazine's website (we did a huge one a couple of years ago on body image). Sarah agreed that friendship would be a great topic for a book, so her team posted the survey in December 2006. A massive 3600 girls filled in the survey and nearly all of you wrote something from the heart about what friendship means to you – delivering us an incredible 160,000 words!

This book is a celebration of the power of friendship. It's an ode to platonic love, the feelings you share with some of the most important people in the world – your friends. As you read on you'll see your words (or at least the words of your generation) in print and from some high-profile women and celebs about the impact friendships have had on their lives, too. This book also includes some fun exercises, affirmations and quizzes to help you improve your friendship smarts and boost your friendship karma. And finally, I've included some expert advice from amazing professionals such as Professor David Bennett, Head of the NSW Centre for the Advancement of Adolescent Health, The Children's Hospital at Westmead and Dr Tim Sharp from the Happiness Institute.

The Friendship Survey we ran in *Girlfriend* magazine showed that 80 per cent of you are happy with your friendships! YAY! Congratulations girls, you're rockin' in the relationship department! It also showed that 80 per cent of you have a best friend. Isn't that cool, you're getting the good vibes from your besties. Sadly, it also showed that 63 per cent of you have been teased by your friends. That statistic really bothered me and was one of the things that prompted me to write this book – my mission is to bust open what I call 'mean-girl culture'. It's really important to understand that good friends may jest with each other, joke around and jibe each other in a fun way, but teasing each other is simply *not* OK. The fact that 63 per cent of girls have been hurt by their friends is something I want to change and I know you do too! Let's help each other and find ways to combat this worrying trend.

Mostly, *GirlForce Friends* is about taking time out from your busy schedules to have fun, and read about, and interact with, girls of your generation. This is an awesome snapshot of who you are as a group – and it's really powerful. I was inspired by your words, sometimes deeply troubled by what you wrote too, but I was ultimately uplifted by your honesty, insight, integrity and courage. Thank you for sharing your heartfelt feelings with me and the girls of your world.

Sadly, I didn't have room to publish every single one of your responses. What I did in the end was pick comments that represented feelings, experiences and ideas that many of you expressed over and over. I'm certain you will relate to much of what we've published. (If your words didn't appear here keep an eye on our website *www.girlforce.com.au* because we'll post many comments there over the coming weeks and months.)

Humans are sociable beings. Without friends we get depressed, sick and sometimes even die. Friendship is as essential to a happy, healthy life as good food, water and shelter are, so we should never take it for granted. It doesn't really matter if you haven't got hundreds of friends, but it matters a lot if you haven't got any. This book will help you make new friends if you don't have friends now and it will give you the tools and compassion to improve the relationships you've got. Read on and discover all the secrets to happy, healthy and harmonious relationships.

Love

Best friends *forever*

2 gether

4 eva

How to make great friendships even better

Where would we be without our friends? Our friends love us for who we are. They make us laugh. They allow us to share our secret thoughts. They get our bad jokes. They support us and advise us. They cheer us on when we win and pick us up when we're blue. They're our friends and we love them. They make us whole and happy.

A good life is a life that's shared with others. This book is all about improving your friendship karma (even if you are a great friend and have amazing friendships we can all do better in the relationship stakes sometimes). You're going to learn how to create boundaries, discover how to communicate your needs more effectively, work out when to give each other space and how to effectively support each other through the highs and lows of life.

Sound good? If you wanna create lasting friendships that will nourish your soul and set your spirits soaring, then read on! You're about to get a whole lot smarter about relationships.

'Everyone needs at least one special friend. Without them, life can seem a whole lot harder. Mine are as close as you come to perfect at my age. We love each other so much. That also includes boys too. It's a great feeling to be able to go up to your friends, girls or boys, no matter where you are and hang your arm around their shoulders and have a huge laugh about your, or their, latest embarrassing moment. We support each other but still keep our values and still stand up for ourselves and beliefs. That's what it's all about.' Kelsie, 12

Wanna create friendships that will last for life?

Here's how

If there is one single thing you can do to ensure that you maintain good relationships forever, it would be to cherish your friends. This means loving them unconditionally. That means being grateful for every day that they're in your life, and celebrating them as people – weaknesses and strengths and everything in between. You'll need to find a place in your heart, which is open and kind – somewhere between compassion and love – that enables you to remain soft and gentle with people. Ultimately, cherishing your friends is about wishing them well and respecting yourself at the same time. Cherishing your friends doesn't mean you have to do everything they ask of you or put your needs behind theirs all the time.

Sometimes it's not always easy to cherish your friends. Sometimes we are hurt by what our friends say and do. No-one, after all, is perfect. So cherishing our friends can sometimes be about forgiveness, flexibility, forgetting and occasionally about having a thick skin.

Cherishing your friends is really about taking a position in your heart. Allowing yourself to be grateful and keeping a loving space within you so that you don't harden towards your friends – even when they make mistakes.

Cherish the love

The best friendships are those that make you a better person. Maybe the relationship makes you feel better about yourself or encourages you to go beyond your fears. Or maybe you're healed by the unconditional love and acceptance your friend gives you. The idea of a good relationship is that you grow as a result of your mutual love and respect.

Cherishing a friend means you need to put all judgement aside. And that's not easy! If you want to discover how to love and cherish your friends, do the following meditation to help you discover the bliss that such an open-hearted approach to friendship will give you.

Cherish meditation

Sit down in a quiet room, close your eyes and allow 10 minutes for this meditation. To prepare, put both hands on your stomach and take three deep breaths. On each inhalation, push out your stomach, filling the lower lobes of your lungs with air. As you exhale, feel your stomach relax as the air is expelled from your lungs. After three breaths your body should be relaxed and your mind receptive to the meditation.

See yourself walking in the sunlight along a long and winding path. Ahead of you is a green meadow. Coming across the meadow is your dear friend. You are happy to see your friend and you wave to her/him. Your friend comes over to you and the two of you stand in the green meadow in the sunlight. You turn to face each other and your eyes meet. You stand gazing into each other's eyes for a long time, smiling and just enjoying each other's company. After a while you tell your friend all the qualities you value in them – their courage, their kindness, their beauty, their sense of humour. They smile and lovingly accept your compliments. Then you tell them that you wish only good for them – prosperity, wisdom, compassion, good health, long life and happiness. Telling them your sincerest wishes for their good fortune fills you with love and energy. Your heart is filled to overbrimming with happiness for your own good fortune to know such a person. The friend thanks you for your well wishes and together you return to the long and winding path. After a time you part ways and you walk alone on the path with a feeling of good luck and good fortune that you have had such an experience.

When you are ready take three deep breaths as before, and slowly and gently open your eyes.

'We moved a lot when I was young so I spent most of my school years being the new kid. It was pretty hard at times and I remember how nervous I used to get before starting a new school. First days were always hideous and it was immediately obvious who the 'cool kids' were. I used to be filled with dread thinking that I wouldn't fit in and scared that no-one would like me. School is unique because it has a very clear and often ruthless social structure and it all seems very serious and important at the time. I often felt awkward because I looked a bit different and I so desperately wanted to be one of the hot blonde girls that all the boys liked.

Usually when starting a new school, it would be the least popular girls who would welcome me with open arms and, at times, I couldn't appreciate it because I was so desperate to climb the social ladder so that I could feel secure. However, as I got older, and the more schools I went to, I started to realise how trivial and pointless all these silly social games were. Every school had the same problems, there were some people who were extremely popular, some who weren't, bullies, those who were bullied... the list goes on. I became less concerned with being accepted and started to really appreciate people for who they were and stopped caring about fitting in, which made me so much happier and secure in myself. I learned that the more you know yourself and are comfortable and happy with who you are, the better friend you can be to everyone.

I have been out of school for some time now and I really appreciate the travel we did because I have friends all over the country whom I love dearly. The social anxiety I felt at school was pointless because once you leave that small community things really change. Some of the most popular people really struggled to find their feet in the world and some of those who were teased ended up being the most successful and inspirational people. I have five girlfriends that I met in my last high school and we have all been friends for over twenty years (which is a bit scary). We are all so different but we are there for each other no matter what. We have all made mistakes, had our ups and downs, fought over big things and little things but we have always stuck together and always will. That's all that matters in the end.'

Pia Miranda, actress

Are you happy with your friendships?
Yes   89%   No   11%

Have you got a best friend?
Yes   80%   No   20%

Are you in a group?
Yes   92%   No   8%

Friends change

One thing you really need to know about friendship is that it's dynamic – it changes. Your challenge as a friend is to adapt to those changes and flow with them. During this phase of your life you'll notice your friends change at an incredibly rapid pace. Some of those changes will be small, like shifting her crush from week to week, but other changes will be bigger, like your best friend suddenly ditches her whole group of friends that she's known since kindergarten and takes up with a new posse. The trick is to find ways to give your friends the space to change while at the same time keeping the essential threads that bind you together. Sometimes that means allowing your friends to make mistakes and sometimes that will mean allowing yourself to make mistakes.

Often you'll discover that you're the one who's changing while your friends are not. Maybe your values have changed – you're ready for a boyfriend while they're still into girlie sleep-overs, you're ready to take schoolwork more seriously while your friends are all goofing around in class. Whatever the circumstances, this is a phase in your life where it's easy to get out of step with your friends and find yourself feeling alone.

From the weekly forums run over the past few years, I've gathered some of the questions that came up about changing friendships. My answers will help you to come to grips with some of these issues around the changing nature of friendship.

My best friend has recently got a boyfriend and is spending all her time with him. What should I do?

My advice is to give her space to explore the relationship. Even though it's very painful for you to step aside, it's important that she learns how to relate to boys and discovers intimacy with the opposite sex. Your job, as a friend, is to support her choices and be there through the highs and lows of the relationship. The chances are that after the initial excitement dies down she will end up spending more time with you and will want to confide in you about her experiences. When you're ready you'll need her to do the same for you – and who knows, you may learn from her relationships with guys?

I've had a best friend all the way through school and we've spent a lot of time together, just the two of us, but I am now finding that I want to spread my wings. What do I do? I don't want to hurt her, but I want to meet new people, too.

My best suggestion would be to somehow incorporate her into a new and expanded group. I would start by encouraging her to expand her friendship horizons and see how open she is to loosening her ties to you and opening herself up to new friendships. It's a lovely thing to have a best friend, as long as she's not preventing you from growing and changing, and experiencing new relationships. Work on her confidence by encouraging her and see if you can help her feel secure enough to widen her circle.

Recently my friend has become obsessed with getting a boyfriend. It's all she talks about! Sure, I want a boyfriend one day, but it's not the be-all-and-end-all of my world! I'm getting annoyed. What should I do?

Unfortunately for you your friend's hormones are taking over her brain and making her obsess about boys. It's perfectly normal, and it can also be irritating for you when you're not thinking and feeling the same way. My suggestion would be for you not to take it too seriously. Getting hot under the collar about boys is part and parcel of growing up, and many girls, and boys, go through this phase (it could happen to you too!). Just accept that this is a phase she'll get over and find ways to just have fun with it.

I'm really small for my age and I haven't got boobs or my period yet. All my friends are really developed and they look years older than me and they kind of put me down for looking young. What should I do?

This is a challenging time because we all grow and develop at different rates. Some 12 year olds look 16 and some 16 year olds look 20. At the same time, some 16 year olds look 12! If your friends are real friends they won't put you down or make judgements about the way you look. Real friends support each other. It may be time for you to widen your circle of friends? Maybe join a club or a sport where you can meet new people? In time you will catch up to your friends, and you will get your period when your body has matured to that point. Try not to worry. You are perfectly normal and not alone. Many girls experience the same issues as you.

Question: I'm not one of the popular girls. How can I get more people to like me and for me to be more cool?

The answer is simple, but it takes a bit of work to achieve. The key is to like yourself first. If you like yourself, and stop judging yourself, comparing yourself to others and putting yourself down, you will attract people because you're feeling confident and happy in your own skin. Also, if you like yourself you won't worry whether people think you are cool or not – you'll be happy with attracting the right friends to you whether they are popular or not. Don't strive to be in the popular group, strive to improve your self-esteem and you will naturally attract friends. Do this affirmation every day: 'I accept and love myself just the way I am. I naturally attract loving and caring friends who accept me as I am.'

'As I've learned through the years, like boys, friends come and go. Although friendships last longer than boyfriends. It's just that as the years go by everything like situations, people, morals and attitudes change. This causes friendships to drift apart and your friends are no longer the same people that they were a year ago. Even though this happened a lot as I was growing up, I've found that there's no point making it a messy break-up, it's just better to accept that things change and focus on all the good times that you had with them rather than making it into something really nasty and bitchy'.

Brizzy, 18

The qualities that create good friendship karma

If being a perfect friend came naturally to us all of the time then the world would probably be a better place. But it would certainly be pretty boring and we'd all be in a state of suspended animation where nothing changed or grew. The upside of the challenges that friendships present us with is that challenge makes us grow and change.

The truth is that being a good friend is something we generally have to work at. And when we work at things, we grow and develop as a person. Of course there are times when your friendships are all wonderful, and you feel great about life, but there are also times when you can feel down in the dumps about your friends (or lack of friends) and it's these times when it comes in handy to remember that we must work on ourselves first if we want to enjoy the fruits of friendship.

Cultivate these qualities in yourself and watch your friendships bloom and grow.

It may sound like an old-fashioned word, but the key to long-lasting relationships is respect. The trick to building respect into friendship is that you need to respect yourself as much as you respect your friends. There's a saying 'You teach people how to treat you,' which really means that other people respond to the signals we give them. If you allow yourself to be treated badly or treat yourself badly, other people will sense it and treat you accordingly.

So what exactly is self-respect? Self-respect is a psychological state that involves thinking, feeling and behaving in ways that reflect an inner ability to accept, trust and believe in yourself. Yes, it's about liking yourself as a person, but it's also about accepting that you can live comfortably with your strengths and your weaknesses. Trusting yourself means knowing that you can cope with whatever life throws at you and believing in yourself means you have the confidence to create what you need to fulfil your hopes and dreams. Ultimately, self-respect is about knowing you are a valuable and worthwhile person.

Self-respect

'Just because you think you have everything right in your pocket, don't take it for granted!! I did and I lost many of my friends because I didn't put much work into the friendship. Always treat your friends with respect and behave the way you want to be treated!!' Kim, 15

When you respect yourself it usually follows that you are capable of respecting others (and it works in reverse too, those with a low sense of self-respect generally have a low regard or respect for others). The basis of good friendship is mutual respect – that means:

★ You appreciate their opinions.
★ You respect their personal space and values.
★ You respect their decisions.
★ You don't judge one another for being different.
★ You celebrate your differences as well as your similarities.
★ You treat each other in loving, generous and considerate ways.
★ You don't put each other down.
★ You know what's important to them.
★ You never degrade each other in any way.
★ You don't gossip about each other.
★ You share in decisions.
★ You aim to be the best person you can be together and apart.

If you have a low sense of self-respect it's important to try to build it up, not just because it helps promote healthy and uplifting friendships, but also because self-respect is essential for a healthy and balanced life. Here's how to boost your sense of self-respect:

★ Don't put up with bad treatment of any kind.

★ Practise a daily affirmation such as: 'I love and respect myself and attract love and respect from others.'

★ Do regular exercise – it reduces stress, boosts self-esteem and promotes harmony in the body and mind.

★ Do something kind for yourself every week such giving yourself a pampering treatment – always raises your spirits.

★ Remember your feelings and opinions matter – don't be dominated by others.

★ Show the world you like yourself by maintaining good grooming – nothing highlights low self-esteem like unkempt hair and nails, drab clothes and drooping shoulders. Tame your mane, glam up your look and flash your best features; you will show everyone that you not only like yourself, but you willpositively shine.

Compassion is an internal state of mind where you make an effort to empathise with other people and put yourself in their shoes. It involves asking yourself, 'I wonder how she feels about her parents getting divorced?', 'I wonder how he feels when he's being bullied?' Compassion is a feeling of caring for other people's wellbeing. Basically it's about giving a damn! In the Buddhist sense, compassion can be roughly defined in terms of a state of mind that is non-violent, non-harming and non-aggressive. It is a mental attitude based on the wish for others to be free of their suffering. Without compassion, there would be no real friendship.

Compassion

Compassion allows you to deeply care for and about others.

When I was 16, I was diagnosed with anorexia nervosa. It wasn't a great day in the history of being me. My mum took me into hospital and all day long I lay in bed just terrified. Not because I was worried about my mental or physical health, hah, I had little care for that. I was just terrified about losing my friends.

I was convinced they'd all hate me because I was weak and stupid because I had this ridiculous illness. So instead of thinking about what was happening, I lay there just going over and over how my friends would never speak to me again and how much I hated myself for getting ill. So imagine my surprise when out of nowhere, just after school got out, one by one my friends started to appear; all shocked and worried but all with eyes of understanding and compassion. No-one judged me. No-one thought I was weak. All of them knew far better than me how little control I had over what was happening to me, and how sick I really was and had nothing but an open heart.

Their acceptance of me and what was happening changed the course of my life forever. So, I know this might sound lame, but I hope that if you have a friend who stumbles like I did, that you will have the courage and heart to hold out your hand like these wise young girls. To know it is not your job as a friend to fix them, or make their problems go away, but to just to let them know you are there and you accept them; to be their friend.

Sancia Robinson, author/producer

'I think it is important to have friends from all different backgrounds. No-one opinion is correct and the more people's opinions and stories you hear and listen to, the more it will help teach you understanding. When you take time to understand why a friend feels the way they do, you won't feel the need to bitch about them, you may even begin to respect their actions.' Anonymous

If you look up the dictionary definition of the word 'honesty' you'll find that it means: 'A quality of fact or being honest; upright or fairness, sincerity or frankness'. This literal definition is useful when we're talking about friendship because it is important to tell the truth to your friends. Honesty builds trust and respect between friends and allows you to know where you stand with someone.

Honesty and trust go hand in hand. Friends don't lie to each other and they don't fake it with one another. Friends are authentic with their words and deeds. Honesty builds trust and trust builds honesty, these two qualities are like pillars that support the house of friendship. Any breach in either honesty or trust can send a friendship crashing down.

Being honest doesn't mean you have to tell your friends everything. You don't have to spill all your most personal secrets and you also don't have to give voice to every opinion or thought that pops into your head. It's important to learn the difference between being kind and discreet and using honesty as a weapon to hurt someone. Just because you have an opinion about the way a friend dresses, or what you really think of her boyfriend doesn't mean you need to share it or air it in public – honesty is about being authentic and truthful, not about telling your friends what you think about them 24/7.

Learn to discriminate between a friend who is truthful, faithful and upfront, and a friend who is dishonest.

'A friendship is the most important thing in the world. Like any other relationship it is a two-way street. Remember a good friendship excludes selfishness, bitchiness and dishonesty.' Amy, 16

Honest friends

⚡ Share information without playing games.

⚡ Are discreet about your secrets.

⚡ Only offer an opinion when it's asked.

⚡ Tell the truth without hurting.

⚡ Don't talk behind your back.

⚡ Don't gossip.

⚡ Share possessions, time, kindness, compassion, respect and intimacies freely.

⚡ Use discrimination and ethical judgement in what they say and do.

⚡ Give you compliments without fake flattery.

⚡ Are authentic and genuine in the way they talk to you.

Dishonest friends

⚡ Play games with information – sometimes withholding and sometimes sharing when it suits them.

⚡ Spill your secrets to others.

⚡ Give you their opinions on how you dress, what you like, your friends, your choices and present it as 'honesty' when it somehow hurts you. For example: 'I'm just being honest but your bum looks big in that dress'. A good friend would steer you away from a fashion mistake by coaching you to wear something else without putting you down in the process.

⚡ Gossip and spread lies about you.

⚡ Withhold time, possessions, intimacies, respect, compassion, kindness and friendship.

⚡ Offer fake flattery in the place of genuine compliments.

⚡ Are inauthentic and disingenuous, false, hypocritical and unkind.

Intimacy

When you have trust, honesty and compassion in a relationship you can build intimacy. Intimacy is where you have created a bond of deep trust allowing to share your most personal thoughts, feelings and experiences. If honesty and trust are the pillars that hold up the house of friendship, intimacy is the wallpaper and window-dressing – it's the thing that makes friendship sweet, magical and meaningful.

There is nothing more beautiful than a secret shared with a friend, a private laugh or the knowledge that there is someone special that you can turn to when the chips are down. Intimacy is an essential ingredient in all great friendships and it's the deepest, sweetest, most cherished aspect of being close to someone.

How do I possibly place into words something that overwhelms my every emotion?

You, my friend, cannot be described, measured or summarised by the spattering of a few words on paper.

For every word evokes hundreds of memories and smiles and as I begin to write them I start to remember hundreds more…

The endless conversation, giggles, and adventures we have embarked upon, priceless advice and your unconditional love and support has awakened my soul and opened my heart.

Here in the silence you sit beside me already knowing what I'm thinking, dreaming and hoping for.

You have shared my happiness, divided my sorrow and walked beside me when I have needed you.

What can I say, friend, but thank you for being you and loving me for me.

Tara Rushton, actress

Sharing

You'll find if you're open and generous and loving your friends will respond in a similar way and your life will be filled with gifts.

When you were a little kid you learned that it was important to share your toys. As you have grown into a young woman you've discovered that it's fun to share your clothes, makeup, accessories. Most importantly, you've also discovered that one of the essential keys to a great friendship is sharing yourself. Sharing yourself means you are generous with your time and your innermost thoughts and feelings. It's not about spilling every secret you've ever had, but it is about feeling safe enough with your friends to trust them with the things that matter to you. You can't have intimacy without sharing yourself. You can't have that delicious sense of 'we' without sharing yourself.

Sharing is about nurturing trust in a relationship and it's vital to creating a close bond with someone. It's true that, at times, it's powerful to withhold from friends – whether that's time, money, space, personal belongings, thoughts, feelings, ideas, etc. And girls can be masterful at withholding – we all know how it feels to have something withheld or feel excluded from what's going on. But this withholding runs counter to the whole idea of creating and building close bonds with people. So it's important to know when it's appropriate to hold something back and when that holding back is used as a weapon.

'One quote which perfectly describes my relationships with my best friends is as follows. "Your friends will know you better in the first minute you meet than your acquaintances will know you in a thousand years", (from Jonathan Livingston Seagull by Richard Bach.)' Amanda, 20

There's an old truism, 'patience is a virtue', but it's not just a virtue in life, it's a virtue in friendships as well. Everyone grows and evolves at a different rate. It's especially obvious during the teen years while you're trying to find your own voice and personality among a changing tide of hormones, peer pressure, school pressure and parental expectations. In friendships, it's really important to learn how to respect your friend's evolution and be patient about the changes you are all experiencing.

Patience

'I must say the year 2006 has made me realise who my real friends are. We, my group of friends, were so close back in 2004. When 2006 hit, it all turned into a roller-coaster ride for me and my friends. Honestly, we are growing apart from each other and we realise it and have tried to keep the friendship, but I guess when ego controls your mind, nothing will happen. We just keep on growing apart. All of us, we don't hang out together, share secrets, call, text each other any more. But it has made me realise who my true friends are, which is very few of them. Girls can be really mean to each other and god knows why? I am thankful to have a best friend who has/ will always be there. We've been through a lot - arguments about friends, clothes, even a boyfriend, - but we realise that we can't live without each other's support. I love her for that.' Eleena, 16

Kindness

The pop star Annie Lennox said, 'Ask yourself: Have you been kind today? Make kindness your daily *modus operandi* and change your world.' Where would we be without kindness? Kindness oils the wheels of all relationships. A gift of time, a thoughtful present or a laugh can change a person's life. Kindness is about giving of yourself. It's a gift that your friends will cherish and remember. Kindness is about thinking of others. It involves taking yourself away from your own thoughts and commitments and asking yourself, 'What can I do to make someone else happy? Being kind to our friends means making allowances for their faults, failures and weaknesses. It means giving them time. It means supporting them and being open and honest with them. Sometimes being kind to a friend means giving them tough love too, such as when they are hurting themselves in some way. Kindness means giving others your unconditional love and showing them your best self. Kindness can mean being generous, but that's not the biggest part of kindness — kindness is really the ongoing appreciation we have for our friends and showing them our love.

A good friend displays kindness, loyalty, truthfulness and love to everyone.' Lucy, 12

You're deadlocked. Neither of you can see the other's point of view. Then one of you cracks a joke and both of you fall about laughing. Humour is one of the most important tools in your friendship kitbag. Being able to laugh at a situation, being able to see the light side of an issue, as well as the serious side, can be the very thing you need to resolve conflicts and bring you closer. Having a sense of humour is not just about telling bad jokes (and it's never about making jokes at another person's expense) it's about being able to laugh at yourself and with your friends. Not taking yourself too seriously and being able to view life through the prism of humour is a great gift to relationships.

> **Laughter is the closest distance between two people.**
>
> Victor Borge (1909–2000), musician

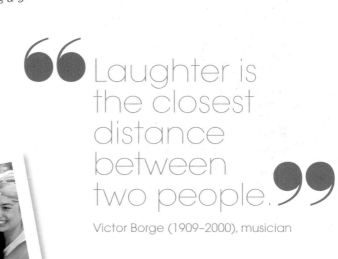

Humour

Secrets to building positive relationships

C = Clarity
(of goals, direction and life purpose)

If you want to be happy with others you need to be happy with yourself first. The first step is to have clear goals and outline an action plan to meet those goals. Be clear about what you want from your life right now (and remember no-one else can do it for you).

H = Healthy living
(activity and exercise, diet and nutrition, and sleep)

Your health is something you may take for granted but it's a crucial part of the foundation of happiness. It's hard to be happy if you're literally sick and tired all the time. So do whatever you can to be healthy and fit – that way you'll boost your chances of being happy.

O = Optimism
(positive but realistic thinking)

There's no doubt that happy people think about themselves, others and the world differently. Among other things, they search for more positives. The good news is that this is something you can learn to do so start practising now.

C   H   O

The key to happy and harmonious relationships is being happy with yourself. Dr Tim Sharp, the director of the Happiness Institute says,

'I believe that happiness is something you CHOOSE. At the Happiness Institute we use this acronym for the six key things we believe lead to happiness and ultimately happy relationships'.

Here are Dr Tim's key things to help you love and accept yourself – so you can love and respect others. As you can see, within this acronym, the second 'O' stands for 'Others', or all the relationships in our lives, and there's absolutely no doubt that happy people have good relationships.

O = Others
(the key relationships in your life)

Research shows that happy people have both more and better quality relationships. So make sure you devote time to developing and nurturing your key relationships.

S = Strengths
(your core qualities)

Rather than spending all their time trying to 'fix' their 'weaknesses', happy people spend more time identifying and utilising their strengths. Find out what you're good at and do it as much as possible.

E = Enjoy the moment
(live in, and appreciate the present)

The past is history, tomorrow's a mystery and today's a gift – that's why they call it 'the present'. Live in the moment and enjoy life more.

O S E

Dr Tim also says, 'I believe that good quality positive relationships are based on 'SUPPORT'. Here's another helpful acronym where each of the letters in 'SUPPORT' stands for a key relationship concept.

S = Strengths

Look for, and appreciate them in others. Don't just tolerate but embrace the differences among your family and friends.

U = Unconditional positive regard

Unless you have proof otherwise, approach each relationship and each interaction with a belief that the other person is good and that the relationship and interaction will be positive.

P = Purpose

Think carefully about the purpose of your relationships. Every relationship and every interaction is different. Not all relationships are the same. For example, you don't need to be as intimate with every person in your life the way you are with your best friend or your family. Find a place and purpose for each relationship.

P = Praise and positivity

This one's simple, give praise and be positive as much and as often as possible!

O = Open communication

Be sincere and authentic and let others know what you're thinking (in an assertive and appropriate way). Don't expect them to read your mind and/or to automatically know what you're feeling (and don't do the same yourself).

R = Respect

Any and all good relationships depend on respect and, as you can see below, trust. Respect is about appreciating people's differences without judgement and allowing them to be who they are.

T = Trust

An essential ingredient in any good relationship, trust is about knowing that you are safe with another person, knowing you are not being judged for being who you are and knowing that your intimate thoughts and feelings are respected by that person.

O R T

This model really works. But like anything, you need to make it work by practising the ideas' here. When you are struggling with an aspect of a relationship, try to remember these acronyms and you'll find a simple method of getting to the heart of the issue quickly.

You're so close you know everything about each other. You know her dreams and desires and the hot guy she craves. Do this quiz and check out how much secret stuff you know about each other.

1. Her favourite colour is?

2. Her middle name is?

3. Her favourite food is?

4. Her fave actress is?

5. Her fave actor is?

6. Her all-time favourite CD is?

7. The last time she cried was?

8. Her favourite thing to do on a Saturday afternoon is?

9. Her favourite animal is?

10. Her dress size is?

11. The name of her latest crush is?

12. She's most afraid of?

13. When she leaves school she's gonna be a?

14. Her finest achievement to date is?

15. The thing that would most embarrass her is?

16. If she had $100 in her pocket she'd spend it on?

17. Her favourite kind of weather is?

18. She gets grumpy when?

19. I could make her happy by?

20. The thing that would hurt her most is?

21. Her favourite thing in her wardrobe is?

22. The part of her body she likes most is?

23. The part of her body she likes least is?

24. Her fave TV show is?

25. Her most treasured possession in the world is?

Are you soul sisters?

Scoring

Fill out the questions with your answers and get your bestie to do the scoring. (Ramp up the fun-factor by filling out the answers for each other at the same time). Each correct answer scores a 1.

0–10 Skimming the surface

You may think you and your friend are close but you don't know enough about her to claim bestie status. It may be that you don't know – yet – how to develop intimacy with a friend, or it may be that you're still on a get-to-know-each-other footing. Either way, you need time to allow this relationship to grow and develop. It's possible you (or she) may have an issue with trust. If you've been teased or bullied or abused emotionally in any way you might have difficulty connecting. You don't need to quiz her on every aspect of her personal life to become close friends. In time you'll discover that intimacies are shared between friends in a natural and easy way. Nurture your listening skills. Be patient and be interested in her and pretty soon you'll have a deep connection.

11–17 Friends indeed

You guys know each other very well. You're mates in the true sense of the word. You hang around together and share lots of secret stuff. You've learned how to trust one another and you know deep intimacies about each other's hopes and dreams. If she came to you in a crisis she'd know she'd get your undivided attention and unconditional support. If you stay on this path you will have a close friendship that may last a lifetime. You're also not so close that you suffocate each other. You've worked out a happy medium between being a friend and being in each other's faces.

18–25 Best friends

You really are best friends. You are in the lucky position of having met a friend who really connects with you – heart and soul. Your intensity is a beautiful thing but you also have to be careful not to alienate others or create an exclusive club that includes just the two of you. OK, so you feel you don't need anyone else, it's still wise to have a wide and diverse circle of friends that includes lots of people with varying interests and talents. This kind of friendship should be treasured – it doesn't come along too often. However, it can also be stifling and restrictive, especially if one of you cools in your affections before the other. Make sure you maintain some personal space and learn how to have fun with and without each other.

We all like people who make us feel good about ourselves, but challenging friends can teach us a lot too. It's worth asking yourself what kind of friend you are.

Find a quiet place. Give yourself half an hour and consider these questions:

1. Out of ten how important is friendship to you?

2. Do you feel you have enough friends?

3. Do you have one special friend? And if not, how do you feel about that?

4. Which ways could you be a better friend to others?

5. Do you expect too much or too little of your friends?

6. What qualities do you most value in a friend?

7. Which of your relationships could be improved?

8. What actions could you take today to improve that relationship?

9. How could you improve yourself to be a better friend?

10. What qualities do you possess that make you a good friend?

What kind of friend are you?

'My friendships are wonderful and unique. I have the bestest best friend ever! I can always rely on her to be there when I need her. We have our ups and downs but at the end of the day we are still there for each other. Girls and boys are important in my life and both are perfect as friends. My friends bring out different sides of me and with different friends I can talk about different problems. I can talk to my guy friends about practically anything when I just need to express myself but with my girls I can say anything and they will be able to support me and help me. Without my boys, girls, friends and best friend I really don't know where I would be so thank you... Luv you all xoxo' Joyann

Discrimination and judgement

One of the most challenging aspects of relationships is working out when it's appropriate to make judgements about another person for your own good. There's a profound difference between gossiping and bitching behind a person's back, and genuinely working out when a relationship is not working for you.

What you're about to learn is how to acknowledge and tame your dark side (which is often the cause of much bullying and bitchiness), how to handle bullying, negotiate boundaries and pull yourself out of a toxic relationship if you need to.

One of the consequences of setting your own set of moral standards and limits is that it becomes very clear when friends are behaving in ways that are not acceptable to you. Once you set up a code, contract or charter of friendship you then have a standard by which you can judge a person's behaviour. Don't be rigid about the 'rules', but do be clear with your friends about what's acceptable, loving and uplifting behaviour — and what's not.

The rocky road of friendship:

what to do when things go wrong

Friendship ground rules

No-one steps onto a netball court or a hockey field and expects to play at a high level without knowing the rules, yet that's what we expect from relationships every day. We expect that we're going to be brilliant at getting our needs met, being heard, knowing how much to tell, letting someone know when they've crossed a boundary and sharing our innermost thoughts and feelings without being fully equipped to do it. Healthy, balanced, harmonious relationships need a set of rules for engagement in order to thrive and adapt to life's ups and downs.

In the Friendship Survey we did with *Girlfriend* magazine online in January 2007, many of you shared that you and your group have a set of rules by which you all co-exist, but many of you have not had the courage, understanding or experience to put in motion a set of rules for engagement.

This doesn't have to be too serious or hardcore, but what you need – for yourself at least – is a set of rules that impose a standard of how you'd like to be treated and how you should treat each other. This list allows you to quickly work out the difference between a good friend and a toxic friend and serve as a reminder of how important it is for you to treat each other with respect, kindness, love, compassion and humour. I suggest you and your group write up your own 'Friendship Rules', but here's a guideline to get you thinking.

Friendship Rules

- Listen to each other.
- Laugh with each other.
- Discuss things openly without pointing the finger or blaming one another.
- Love each other unconditionally.
- Give our time to each other.
- Cheer each other on.
- Celebrate our friend's achievements.
- Pick each other up when we're down.
- Encourage other relationships with people outside our group.
- Allow each other to express ourselves in different ways – such as through dressing differently or liking different music.
- Accept each other for who we are.

What our group doesn't do is:

- Laugh at each other in a cruel way.
- Tease one another
- Talk behind each other's backs.
- Gossip about each other.
- Take sides in an argument.
- Undermine each other.
- Bring up the flaws of others in the group.
- Compete in unhealthy ways.
- Prevent new relationships forming outside the group.
- Encourage self-destructive behaviours such as smoking, drinking too much, experimenting with drugs.
- Bully each other.
- Deliberately hurt each other.
- Take pleasure in each other's failures or misfortunes.
- Judge each other for who we are.
- Encourage other people to be mean to another member of the group.

Negotiating boundaries

Writing up 'friendship rules' is a great step towards creating harmony within your group because everyone becomes aware of the ground rules. But being in relationships with other girls (and boys) can challenge your personal boundaries every day. A boundary is a personal position or a limit you have on a particular issue or action. A boundary can be as simple as your feelings about right and wrong, or it can be your moral standpoint or your values. For example, a boundary for you may be that it's not OK to tell racist jokes in your presence or it's not OK for your bestie to tell you that you look skanky in a particular outfit.

When someone crosses a personal boundary you have choices about how to deal with it. You can either speak up and voice your upset, by saying: 'Hey, that crosses a line with me. Please don't say that again.' Or, you can simply walk away. Or, if you're particularly skilful, you could use humour to diffuse it, but still let the person know you are uncomfortable. The problem for most teenagers is that they don't really know what their personal boundaries are, so you get crushed a lot without understanding why – you just end up feeling bad about yourself, or the situation.

What you need to do is work out your personal boundaries. (I suggest writing these boundaries down in a journal, diary or even your blog.) Then , once they're committed to paper, follow these guidelines for how to negotiate better boundaries with your friends.

Step 1

Negotiating your boundaries is not about beating the other person into submission so they 'get' your personal boundaries. It's about finding gentle but persuasive ways to get your needs met and get respect for your ethical positions. It usually starts with a statement that declares your position on a particular point. For example, 'Perhaps you didn't mean to say such a cruel thing to me, but it hurt and it's not OK with me for you to speak to me in that way'.

Once you've stated your position it's really important to follow this up with a request of the other person. For example, 'In future would you please not say those sorts of things to me'. What you're doing here is asking the other person to take responsibility for their actions or words.

Step 2

Step 3

It's important for you to support your own position by honouring what you've said. That means you have to mean it. If you ask someone to treat you properly you have to follow through with your own actions – if you're being bullied, report it, don't suffer in silence; if you're being victimised by someone in your group don't just take it, take action against it by taking a stand. Be careful to use this tool wisely, you want to create a win-win situation for both parties rather than humiliate or harass the other person.

"

Friends are incredibly important, but it's not always easy to pick the people who will be true friends. And it's devastating when someone that you thought was on your side lets you down.

Generally, a really good friend is one that actively supports you, not just with words, but with actions. Someone who makes sure you're OK and safe, someone who guards your secrets, and keeps a close watch on your heart.

You are a good person who deserves to be treated well. Don't let people walk all over you. Draw boundaries, and if people cross those boundaries, let them go.

If things get too much, give yourself the same advice you would give your best friend – and take it. No-one will ever know you as well as you know yourself, and your instincts will usually be right. You can't be a good friend to anyone else if you're not a good friend to yourself.

Noni Hazlehurst, actress

"

Do you know how to say 'No'?

1. Your best bud wants to go to the beach but it's that time of the month and you really don't feel like strutting your stuff at the beach. Do you:
   a) Say you're busy (a little white lie won't hurt anyone).
   b) Say 'yes' because she's your bud and she asked you.
   c) Tell her the truth that you're just not feeling like it today.

2. You're at a party and everyone in your gang is smoking. Do you:
   a) Say 'no', walk away disgusted you're OK with not being one of the crowd.
   b) Feel the heat and even though you're not comfortable about it you eventually cave in and join them.
   c) Join the group but manage somehow not to smoke with them.

3. One of the girls in your group is dishing the dirt on your bestie. Do you:
   a) Speak up for her and demand that the girl stops gossiping.
   b) Not say anything but feel bad inside about it.
   c) You don't want to feel left out of the group so you join in.

4. You are primed and ready for a hot date but when he arrives to pick you up you can smell alcohol. Do you:
   a) Ignore it, it's none of your business what he does in his spare time.
   b) Ask him straightaway if he's been drinking and how much. There's no way you'd go out with someone who is drunk.
   c) Let it go to the keeper but make sure you don't get in a car when he's behind the wheel.

Are you little Miss Yes-All-The-Time or are you someone who is comfortable with the 'N-word'? Discover whether you have good boundaries and communication skills or whether you are a walk-over with your friends?

5. Your best friend is having trouble at home and just lately she's begun taking her angst out on you. Do you:
   a) Mostly ignore it. What's a little dump every now and again between friends?
   b) Call her on it and say you understand that she's stressed but it's NOT OK for her to take her upset out on you.
   c) Cut ties with her immediately. Who needs a confrontation with a friend?

6. Which sweet best describes you?
   a) Marshmallow – I'm a complete softie where my friends are concerned.
   b) Sour strap – I'm both bitter and sweet.
   c) Sherbet – I completely dissolve in any emotional situation.

7. Your best friend wants to get matching tattoos but you know your mum would go ballistic if you got one. Do you:
   a) Get one and hide it from your mum – you can't possibly say 'no' to your bestie.
   b) Discuss it again with your mum and if she says no you comply with your mum's wishes.
   c) Figure that your friend is the lesser of two evils, so rather than risking your mum's fury you tell her that you will get one with her sometime in the future.

Scoring

1. a) 1   b) 0   c) 2
2. a) 2   b) 1   c) 0
3. a) 2   B) 1   c) 0
4. a) 0   b) 2   c) 1
5. a) 0   b) 2   c) 1
6. a) 1   b) 2   c) 0
7. a) 0   b) 2   c) 1

14–10 Babe with Boundaries

You are one cool customer. You have no problems with saying 'No' and you have enough confidence to withstand peer pressure. You are one of those rare friends who is prepared to put your butt on the line and stand up for someone else. Occasionally you can be a bit judgemental, but it's OK to have high moral and ethical standards, so stick to your guns. You are a good negotiator so you should be able to find a way to have a win-win with your friends and make compromises when you need to. Pat yourself on the back for being a girl with good boundaries and communication skills.

10-7 Miss Mushy

You are a softie at heart. You love your friends so much that you sometimes compromise your own good judgement and fall in with the crowd. While you're capable of saying 'No' sometimes you need to do some work with the N-word. Next time your bestie wants to go shopping when you want to go to the movies start with a negotiation. For example say this: 'This time I am prepared to go shopping so long as we agree that it's my turn to choose what we do next time, OK?' You need a bit more confidence to risk your friend's ire and not take offence.

7 and below
Walk-all-over-me Girl

It's fair to say you are backward in coming forward with your friends. You allow your friends to take control. It's time to own up to the fact that you need some help to strengthen your personal power and be confident with it. Maybe you've been bullied or have feelings of low self-worth? Whatever the reason for your poor sense of self, it's time to trade it in for some confidence. Start by practising saying 'No' to your friends in the mirror. Write down a daily affirmation and repeat it often until you feel better about yourself: 'I am a worthwhile person. I deserve to be heard and have my needs met. I do not have to trade my power for security.' Don't let your friends walk-all-over you, you are a valuable person, all you need to do is believe it yourself!

Beating Mean girl culture

The great news is that the Friendship Survey showed that a massive 89 per cent of you are happy with your friendships. That's awesome! About 80 per cent of you also said that you have a best friend – one of the loveliest things a girl can have. And 90 per cent of you said you were friends with boys who weren't your boyfriends. That shows how much the world has changed since your parents were kids – it's a far more equal and democratic world these days!

What was incredibly revealing about your generation, is that a massive 87 per cent of you said there was too much bitchiness at school and 63 per cent of you reported that you had been teased by your friends. Sadly, 34 per cent of girls said they had been forced out of a group and 35 per cent said that most of the upsets in the group were caused by arguments over friends.

While there has always been an element of bitchiness among girls, and bullying has been around since the dawn of time, what I think is new is the way that bitchiness is somehow cool. The way it's presented in the media is that the girl with all the smarts is the one with the sharpest tongue. A put-down is now considered so much a part of conversation that many of us don't even notice when we've been abused.

I am personally really offended by this idea that it's not only OK to slag off at your friends, but that you're cool if you do! I've spoken to hundreds of girls who feel the same way and I'm literally asked every week for strategies on how to combat it.

This book celebrates the beauty of friendship, but it's also designed as a manual for acing up your own friendship karma and beating mean girl culture.

Let's be friends with one another and treat each other with compassion, kindness, soft words and loving gestures.
It's cool to be kind.

'I was kicked out of a clique because I didn't do what I was supposed to. I was bullied for a year and a half before I actually did something about it. When the school counsellor talked to the queen bee, who was bullying me, she said, 'I don't bully, I just demand respect!' She turned friends against me, so now they won't even look at me, and started some really vicious rumours about me. I lost a lot of respect and missed a lot of school because it was too stressful for me to be there. Now she's not even allowed to come near me. She's already replaced me with another girl in the clique, who she orders around and uses. The school still hasn't told her parents she bullied me, which disgusts me because they need to know what their daughter is really like.' Hannah, 15

'Well ... there is this girl at my school called Emma. She always acts so innocent and 'cute', but she is actually a manipulative bully. You see she has 'favourites'. This involves her subconsciously selecting one person out of our group (her new favourite), because she either considers them hilarious, cute or just decides she loves them. She then confides in that person for a few weeks, telling them all about her fabulous boyfriend and everything that happens when she goes on dates with him, or she'll tell them all about how much she hates this person and how much she thinks that person is a bitch etc.

She'll invite them over all the time for sleepovers and to go see her boyfriend. She excludes everyone else in the group when she has "private" conversations For example, if the group was all sitting together eating lunch, she'd stand up, make her favourite stand up, then whisper in her ear, "Come to the locker room with me", then take her hand and run off to the locker room, only to tell her favourite about how excited she is about her date with her boyfriend. And when people stand up to her and say they feel excluded, etc, a massive fight would erupt.

She'd then realise that she was "over" her favourite, find some excuse to ditch them and exclude them from everything. She did this to one of my friends, Sarah. They were practically best friends, when Emma claimed that Sarah was using her (because she realised that she was "over" Sarah). They had this massive fight and all of a sudden Sarah was forced out of the group by Emma. Sarah is not in our group anymore. Emma turned everyone against her. Sarah never comes to the group's social events, and Emma is always bitching about her and how much of a bitch Sarah is. This is the typical cycle of Emma.

I would also like to take this opportunity to talk about another "friend" of mine, Emily. Emily is known for being funny. But recently I have realised that she is actually not that funny and most of her jokes offend others. On the bus on the way to netball training, she randomly said that I, "Always look like a zombie." She then said, "I'm sorry, but it's true... you always have these massive bags under your eyes and you always look dead." This really offended me – she is aware that I am very self-conscious and that I believe myself to be ugly (but I mainly think I'm ugly because of her remarks). What also offended me was that she said it in front of everyone, belittling me and embarrassing me. I felt like I couldn't stand up to her, because I was convinced that what she said was true.

Numerous times, she has also said that I am flat-chested in front of the group. One day she was telling everyone about how she went shopping for a bra with her mum, and how the bra fitted her perfectly. She then said, 'I'm so glad that I can fit into a bra, unlike some unfortunate people,' she then looked at me and said, 'Such as Alice'. Yes, I was aware that my boobs weren't too big, but I didn't need to be embarrassed in front of everyone again. Everyone started laughing after she said that. I didn't know what to do or say. I get so shy when she picks on me.' Alice, 13

Have you ever been cyber-bullied?

Yes 33%
No 67%

Do you think the media promotes a mean girl culture among girls?

Yes 36%
No 64%

Do you think celebrities promote a mean girl culture among girls?

Yes 53%
No 47%

Do you gossip about other girls?

Yes 71%
No 29%

Are you aware of any gossip about you?

Yes 64%
No 36%

Bullying:

it starts with you

Bullying is a form of violence. It's abusive and cruel. No-one likes to be picked on or put down, it hurts, so let's do our best to stamp it out – *now*

Ever wondered why we bully each other? My theory is that we all have a shadow within us, a dark side that falls into negative thoughts about others, and ourselves, and sometimes compels us to act in mean and cruel ways. We all have this shadow and the challenge is to find ways to accept and embrace that dark side of ourselves. From my own perspective, I aim to search out the dark parts in myself, shine a flashlight on them and to bring them into the light. When you are aware of your internal demons you have a better chance of battling with them and winning!Getting control of your shadow is not easy. It takes patience and it takes work. Hunt out your shadow, own it and then work out ways to tame it (or at least lessen the effect it can have on your relationships).

Tame your *dark side*

Ever said something nasty to a friend and wondered to yourself why you were being such a b***h? We all have a dark side, a kind of evil twin that gets grumpy, moody and downright nasty. Discover how to tame your dark side so you can discover balance and improve your relationship karma.

1. When you're down in the dumps are you more likely to be:
   a) Strung out.
   b) Aggressive.
   c) Withdrawn.

2. You've just had a major blow up with your bestie, do you:
   a) Have sleepless nights, worry excessively and feel unable to fix it.
   b) Feel furious and dream about revenge.
   c) Get depressed and comfort-eat or sleep for long periods.

3. Your parents won't let you hang with your friends at a cool club on the weekend. Do you:
   a) Fantasise about running away and disobeying them.
   b) Become confrontational and hope this strategy will make them give in.
   c) Sulk and hide out in your bedroom and think of the psychological torture inflicted on them will punish them for being unreasonable.

4. When it comes to your dark side which celeb do you most identify with?
   a) Rebel without a cause – Avril Lavigne.
   b) Wild girl– Lindsay Lohan.
   c) Moody and broody – Mary-Kate Olsen.

5. Be honest with yourself on this quiz question. What are the least favourite aspects of your personality?
   a) Restless, low self-esteem, insecure at times, flighty, changeable.
   b) Perfectionist, arrogant, aggressive, critical, controlling.
   c) Lazy, procrastinator, sulky, prone to feeling blue.

6. Your biggest challenges are:
   a) Overcoming my fears and anxieties.
   b) Controlling my temper.
   c) Trying to be more positive.

When you can objectively recognise your qualities (and your personal trouble spots) you are more able to see yourself as others do. We all have positive and negative traits in our personalities. The trick is to become aware of these different traits and learn to work with them. It's not about judging yourself; it is about being aware and as a result being in charge of dealing with your emotional states. This is called being in charge of our stuff!

When you're feeling happy and balanced, you're Miss Personality Plus. You're easy to be around, fun, witty, exciting, creative, sensitive and adventurous. But when the dark side of your nature is in full swing you feel insecure, anxious and light-headed, and your friends and family will notice that you're scattered, cutting and dismissive of other people's feelings. Your way of expressing your dark side is to feel insecure and anxious. To keep your inner-cow in check you need plenty of rest and time out to reflect on your moods and feelings. Nurture yourself with long walks on the beach, a gentle yoga session, warm baths and plenty of fun, light and happy times with friends. When you feel balanced and grounded, many of your anxieties will simply melt away.

Mostly a's –
Miss Insecurity

When things are going well for you, you are charm personified. You're a powerful leader, you're playful and magnetic and full of energy and inspiration. However, when your alter-ego is operating, you are aggressive, judgemental, cranky, a bully and pushy.

To keep your nasty side under control, you need to see the light side of life by watching funny movies with your friends, giving yourself lots of pampering treats, such as a gorgeous manicure or massage, cooling off with a lovely long swim, adding new friends to your posse. When you feel cool, relaxed and at ease with yourself you'll notice that many of your more fiery, angry and anguished personality traits can be handled easily.

Mostly b's –
Miss Angry

Mostly c's –
Miss Passive Agressive

When you feel balanced and the universe is in good order, you are generous, compassionate and nurturing. You're the kind of friend everyone craves. You're an artistic, gentle and loving friend and you simply ooze serenity and femininity. When the darker side of your nature is at the wheel, you're withdrawn, sullen, intolerant, lazy and lacklustre. To keep your witchy-woman off her broomstick you need to get up off your butt and get moving. Nothing lifts the spirits like a hard workout. Even if it's not your natural inclination to get out there and exercise, it's the best prescription when you're down in the dumps. When you're super-charged with vitality and energy, you have the power to banish the blues and get a grip on your stress.

'I remember all my school years vividly. I remember being in primary school and having a great cross-section of friends. I grew up in inner-city Melbourne and was really fortunate that my friends were all from completely different cultures and backgrounds. We accepted each other on face value because we were friends– we played and laughed and mucked around together– we stuck up for one another. Mary was Maltese, Rosie was Italian, I had Australian and Chinese friends, kids who were professors' children and kids who lived in the housing commission at the end of the street. What bonded us was the camaraderie of being girls the same age going through the same experiences.

And essentially that is what bonds me to my female relationships today. A sense of looking out for one another. There is a saying I love, 'It's the blokes who'll pat your arse, but it's the women who'll save it.' And even though I have some wonderful male friendships in my life, and absolutely love my husband to bits (he's my best friend), this cliché is true for me.

I also remember arriving at secondary school, terrified, and having this 'tough chic' slam me against a locker and start shoving and harassing me for no reason.

The next thing I remember is bursting into tears, yelling at her for picking on me, and running off to the toilets. Just when I think I'm free, she storms in behind me and bursts into tears as well, and starts telling me about her awful home life and how her dad hits her. Nothing is ever as it seems.

It takes courage and conviction to be one's self. To not have to pick on others to make yourself feel better. It's easy to gossip and character assassinate when I'm feeling bad about myself or a situation. The hard road is to open up, get humble and admit my vulnerabilities. But when I do this, I have the unique opportunity of opening myself up to another human being and experiencing the absolute joy and wonder of true friendship. I have friends today who know all my dirt, all my secrets. Those friendships are irreplaceable. And completely freeing. And there is something truly awesome about a group of girls sticking together. We just have to make sure we don't abuse that power, and let it turn nasty. It's much more fun being a buddy rather than a bitch.'

Bridie Carter, actress

Your dark side is like a wild animal that needs taming. You can't banish it from your psyche, we all have to live with our shadow selves, but we can bring it to heel and get it to do our bidding – rather than the other way around where we are at the mercy of our shadows and allow ourselves to do cruel and nasty things. Here's how to tame your dark side.

- When you feel a dark impulse rise, name it – whether it's anger, cruelty, judging people harshly, being spiteful, gossiping, calling people names, chiming in on other people's cruelty, dumping your moods, spreading negativity, etc – name it for what it is and say, 'This dark feeling expressing itself as – is part of my shadow and it doesn't have power over me, I have power over it!'.

- Love yourself for yourself – don't reject the dark parts of yourself, embrace them as part of your whole self (the bits we disown have power over us).

- Keep a journal of the feelings you experience and keep a track of them.

- Practice compassion – keep your heart open and loving towards all people and be compassionate with yourself.

- Try not to gossip about other people.

- If your dark side gets a grip at a particular time and you are overwhelmed with a negative emotion, experience the feeling, name it, own it and try to stand outside yourself and allow the feeling to pass.

Controlling
the inner bitch

shadow side traits

self-hatred

jealousy

greed

anger

cruelty

hating others

putting down others

insensitivity

envy

lack of empathy

pettiness

lack of compassion

revenge

bitchiness

being argumentative

controlling behaviour

bullying

gossip

meanness

wanting to harm others

viciousness

Toxic relationships

How do I get a grip?

Something that I am asked over and over, is how to recognise a toxic or abusive relationship. Teenage girls are changing and growing so much, and taking in so many new experiences, that it can be challenging to decode the signals your friends are giving you.

Let's start with a definition of a healthy relationship

A healthy relationship is one where both people who share and support each other through the good and bad times. A healthy relationship is one where you can laugh and cry together and feel safe to share your most intimate thoughts and feelings without feeling judged and without competition. A healthy relationship means you cheer each other on, celebrate each other's successes and console each other for your failures and losses. When someone matters a great deal to you and those feelings of trust and respect are returned, you feel confident, happy, whole, balanced and loved.

Sadly, not all relationships work that way despite our best intentions. Some relationships are what I call toxic and can become abusive and destructive. At their worst, toxic relationships can be both psychologically and physically dangerous and you may need help to get out of one.

Here are some key signs of an abusive or toxic relationship.

There is no definitive guide to a toxic relationship as everyone's experience of an abusive relationship is different. Here, Reach Out www.reachout.com.au a website offered by the not-for-profit organisation, Inspire, lists the following behaviours as precursors to an abusive relationship:

★ Possessiveness

★ Checking on you all the time to see where you are, what you're doing and who you're with.

★ Trying to control where you can go and who you can see.

★ Jealousy

★ Accusing you, without good reason, of being unfaithful.

★ Isolating you from your family and friends, often with rude behaviour.

★ Putting you down, either publicly or privately by attacking how smart you are, your looks or capabilities.

★ Constantly comparing you unfavourably with others.

★ Blaming you for all the problems in the relationship.

★ Menace and threats

★ Yelling, sulking and deliberately breaking things that you value.

★ Threatening to use violence against you, your family, friends or even a pet.

★ Saying no-one else will want you.

If any of these behaviours are ringing bells, in other words they happen to you regularly in one or more of your relationships, you may need some help. You need to know it's not OK to be physically threatened or scared in any way, especially if it means you are being bullied into things that make you uncomfortable or unhappy. It's never OK to be put down, dissed, teased or pushed around. And let's be clear, if there's physical violence involved and you're being shoved, hit, slapped, kicked or punched, you are being abused and you need to report it quick smart. No-one deserves to be treated this way. No-one should use violence — or the threat of violence — to make you do what you don't want to do or make you feel bad, worthless, powerless, pointless, victimised or bullied.

Get some HELP ↓

The first thing to do is honour yourself. If your gut instincts are telling you that a relationship is sliding into abuse, trust that instinct and take action. Start by talking to someone you trust – your mum or dad, a family member, friend, family doctor, teacher, school counsellor, your or call the Kids Help Line on 1800 551 800 for confidential advice. Don't feel ashamed or embarrassed, you are not alone and you will be taken seriously.

Relationships are really about learning about yourself. By their very nature friendships change. They have dark times and light times but the constant in every relationship is YOU.

If you can learn how to see relationships as a mirror of yourself and where you're at, you'll be way ahead of the game. Owning up to your own shadow side, the jealousy, competition, comparing and negative thinking that is part and parcel of all relationships, will make relating to others a lot easier. At times we all compare ourselves with our friends and we all feel jealous, but the trick is to see those feelings for what they are and move on.

Don't judge yourself for feeling jealous that your bestie has gorgeous long legs while yours resemble little stumps, don't feel bad that you're an ace on the tennis court while your friend is completely uncoordinated – we all have different qualities and abilities. Our challenge is to celebrate our differences. The best way to loosen the grip that jealousy, competition and the urge to compare ourselves with our friends can have over our relationships is to name it. Say to yourself, 'I'm a bit jealous that Matilda always scores high in English' or 'I feel bad that Jackie always has all the hottest clothes to wear'. Once you've named those shadow emotions you've come a long way to owning them. Put a positive spin on what might be making you feel negative, such as, 'It's OK because I'm good at maths'. Also, remember there are times when your friends will be jealous and want to compete with you! If you sense that a friend is comparing herself unfavourably with you, just be compassionate and reassure her that you're not perfect, nobody is, and that she has lots of great gifts to be grateful for. And finally, remember to give yourself tonnes of affirmation for the things you're good at and the gifts you were given.

Name it and own it – acknowledge your dark feelings, name them and own them to get them out into the open.

Jealousy and competition

Gossip

'I love my friends but I know that every girl bitches about her friends. It's what girls do. We can't help it. If we have a problem with someone we bitch about him or her. But most girls find out what other girls have been saying and when they go and ask the girls who have bitched about them, they back down because they get scared. I know the solution. Don't bitch about your friends it's not cool.'

Rebekah, 15

Gossip is infectious.

Once someone starts gossiping about someone else it's almost impossible not to join in. However, gossip is a form of bullying and abuse.

Talking about people behind their backs is doing them harm. Even when you think you're talking about that person in an effort to help them, you're not, you're simply sharing personal and private information about them to make yourself feel better. Gossip is about reducing another person's status in the group so you, and others, feel better about yourselves. There is no positive spin you can put on gossip. Sure, it's human to share information about each other– the media does it all the time and magazines are devoted to it – but it's not kind, healthy or helpful. Gossip is hard to resist and often the people who do resist it get gossiped about, but it's important to make a stand on gossip and resist the urge to spread the word. Gossip is a form of bullying and we all know in our hearts when we're spreading rumours and when we're genuinely talking about someone in a caring or helpful way. If you're worried about someone' talk to them directly about your concerns, don't talk about them behind their back. And if the talk turns to put downs, insults, making nasty and negative judgements, being cruel about a person and just generally being bitchy, it's your job to make a stand and walk away.

PEER PRESSURE

Peer

It's a normal human instinct to want to fit in. We are programmed with a fight and flight mechanism that goes back to our primitive ancestors who saw a different face as a threat to family and village. This primitive instinct goes some way to explain why we still form little groups or tribes, and do all we can to conform to the rules of our tribe.

If your tribe is into high fashion then you'll probably go all out to get the latest hot outfit to impress your peers. If your tribe is into winning on the sports field you'll probably spend a lot of time training so you can show your tribe that you're strong and capable. There is no other time in your life where it will feel so important to fit in with your group as it does now.

Peer pressure becomes problematic when fitting in becomes so important to you that you are prepared to risk either your physical safety, or your moral compass, to be part of the gang. The classic ways peer pressure effects teenagers is that they experiment with alcohol, cigarettes, drugs, fast cars and general risk taking. But it can also be more subtle ...such as isolating people who don't conform to the strict rules of the group, teasing, bullying and nastiness. There is no way to avoid peer pressure, it's part of growing up – your challenge is to resist the negative aspects of peer pressure so that you are not harmed physically, mentally, emotionally or spiritually. Here are some strategies to help you resist peer pressure.

★ It's OK to say 'No'. This can be very hard when your friends are offering you drugs or alcohol or a fun ride in a fast car, but you need to remember there are consequences for your actions and one of them may be that you or your friends will get hurt. Practise saying no to small things so that when it comes to saying no to a big thing, you're ready for it.

★ It's OK to walk away. When you feel threatened by your peers sometimes the best strategy is to simply walk away. Don't stand and fight the group, they'll usually win en masse. Make your decision and walk away.

★ Try not to worry if they call you a 'dag', 'pathetic' a 'wimp' or a 'woos' – who cares what they think!

★ Remember true friends want the best for you. If someone means you harm or is willing to risk you getting hurt, they are not a real friend.

★ Don't conform to the group's rules if you sense they are wrong. When you turn away from your own internal moral compass you are harming yourself.

Would you do something you are not comfortable doing just because your friends are doing it?
Yes   15%
No   85%

Have your parents ever tried to stop you from being friends with someone?
Yes   44%
No   56%

Are there conflicts in your group?
Yes   28%
No   72%

If there are conflicts in your group, what is the single biggest cause of arguments and upsets (choose one only)
Boys   21%
School   10%
Arguments   35%
over friends
Personal   33%
criticism –
the way you
look or act etc.

How to handle the nasty put-down

Sometimes it comes out of the blue; the bitchy remark or a friendly joke at your expense, sometimes it's a deliberate attack or a blatant backstab. No matter what it is, the nasty put-down is designed to make you feel horrible.

It's true that cattiness is often part and parcel of girl-to-girl relationships, but it doesn't mean you should put up with it. When a put-down comes your way you need to know how to handle it – and fast – because it hurts and the wounds often cut deep.

Sometimes the nastiness is a slag off that comes from someone you don't know, but most often you will know the abuser, and it hurts all the more when you do. It can be your long-time bud who is suddenly threatened because a guy she likes, likes you, or a girl on the edge of your gang who wants to score brownie points by showing she's tougher than you. The insults can be straight up or veiled – an eye-roll when your back is turned or a 'joke' that everyone hears except you. Of course you've been told it's 'Not about you, it's about them.' The abuser is usually insecure, weak and jealous, but it still hurts.

It's important to understand that if someone is trying to put you down it's generally because they've been put down in the past. What the abuser is actually doing is trying to assert their superiority by making you their inferior (psychologists say this is common behaviour for someone who has been put down by authority figures such as parents or teachers). What you need to do next is expose their behaviour – they lose power over you when you confront them face to face (and it doesn't have to get nasty). Finally, you should always report incidents of bullying to a teacher, parent or school counsellor. If you experience the put-down and need some smarts about how to deal, here's how.

1. Stop, take a breath and backtrack by saying something like – 'Hey did you just call me an idiot?'

2. Get them to take responsibility – 'When you joked behind my back what were you really trying to say about me?'

3. Get on the front foot – 'You clearly have a problem with me, let's talk in private.' People who try to embarrass you in front of a group are generally using the group for power. When you get them into a one-on-one situation, they will need to confront their issues with you.

4. Look straight at the abuser – it's much harder for a person to have power over you when you are looking them straight in the face.

5. Take the sting out of the joke with – 'I didn't hear you, can you run that by me again.' It's hard to abuse someone twice and it almost never gets a laugh when you ask someone to repeat it to your face.

6. When you find out something horrible has been said behind your back, go direct to the gossiper and ask them why they said it. If the person confronts it honestly you'll have an opportunity to discuss the problem. If not, and she denies it, just let it go but know that you've put her on notice so she knows you're prepared to tackle it head on.

Verbal assaults are so hard to take because they make you feel helpless and defenceless. They're often random and you can't always work out what you abuser's motives are (sometimes they don't know themselves!) What you do need to know is that you shouldn't put up with a verbal attack – whether it comes from a friendly source or not. It's still a form of abuse and a no-go territory.

How to hear
the hard stuff

We all make mistakes. There's not a person on the planet that can't admit they've gossiped behind someone's back or made a judgemental remark about a friend at an inappropriate time. Most times you won't need to confront your mistake, but occasionally your friend will call you on your crime and you may have to face up to your misdemeanour. The first thing to do is to admit you were wrong and apologise straightaway. The next thing you need to do is own the fact that you're going to feel crummy. And finally, the last thing you need to do is respect the person who is facing you with your mistake and not hit out at them. It is possible that your friendship could be badly affected, but if it is a friendship that is strong and filled with trust, forgiveness will probably be on the cards. Being able to admit you've made a mistake is a powerful step to becoming a person who can take responsibility for their weaknesses as well as their strengths.

Resolving conflict

It's fair to say that during the life cycle of a relationship most friendships experience some form of conflict.

In most cases it will be a little spat over something silly – a misunderstanding, a slight, a joke gone wrong, and so on. In most cases you'll be able to work it out, dust yourselves off and get on with being buddies. However, there are times when it's really difficult to work it out on your own and it may be appropriate either to seek the advice of a counsellor, a parent, teacher or maybe another mature friend who can act as a mediator.

In situations where you're finding that the conflict is taking up a lot of time and energy and creating a great deal of upset, these simple steps may help you.

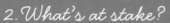

1. Define the dispute

The first step is to pinpoint what the argument is really about and it's a good idea for all or each of you to write down your side of the argument. (It's amazing how differently you may see the conflict from your friend's perspective.)

2. What's at stake?

It's important to discuss the possibility that the friendship is at stake here. If neither of you want to lose the friendship you should agree that you want to make it work and you will do what you can to move forward.

3. Airing each side of the story

Agree that one of you must go first to list any concerns. While the other person is talking try to be impartial and listen with a focused and calm mind.

4. Create a flexible solution that is a win–win one for both of you

Even though it can be really hard to hear the other side of the story, and you will often think your friend has got it all wrong, it's important to be flexible about how you solve the problem. Agree to forgive each other and come from a position of mutual respect. Try not to judge the other person or negate their feelings. It's important to let it go and you may be able to help this situation by giving each other a compliment, writing a lovely note or giving each other flowers.

5. Say sorry and mean it!

It's amazing how powerful an apology can be. Even if you feel you were in the right you can often short circuit an argument by apologising for the upset. You don't have to take the full brunt of the blame but it can be powerful to get on the front foot, own your part of the upset and take responsibility for healing it. When you say sorry cultivate a feeling of genuine compassion in your heart and you will most likely find that the conflict can be settled pretty quickly.

"

The days of school don't seem that long ago for me. Each year brought a new excitement, a new journey, a new challenge. In the early years of my high school life I was incredibly reserved. I had one best friend, but she was moved to another school to start her high school life. So I was faced with the daunting challenge of creating a whole new friend base! I stayed quiet and was in my own little world for most of Year 7. I was fortunate to start a friendship with the 'popular girl' (who is now my closest friend in the world) later that year. We were paired up in woodwork. I was quick to judge her, thinking she was a so-called 'bitch' simply because she was so popular. The absolute wrong thing to do. After a conversation with her, that first and very stupid judgement was thrown out the window – never judge a book by its cover.

From Year 8 onwards the taunts of bullying from girls subtly began. Most of them targeted my friend but because I was her close friend I started to get picked on too. Even threats of violence – for no particular reason for that matter. Just like I had wrongly judged my friend at first impression, I was now being judged from every angle. I remember my folder being scribbled over with horrible things when I accidentally left it in the playground, things being written on the back of toilet doors.

I never understood why I was targeted. It was always girls in older years too. I never went out of my way to fight back, nor did I ever instigate bitchiness or bullying. In fact, I was the opposite. My friend and I had a 'no gossip' rule between us. People deserve a chance to be themselves. We don't need to gossip or bully. If ever we did we were only inviting the universe to reflect it back on our own circumstances and ourselves so instead we just went about our lives no matter what was said about us.

As I grew older I joined the student council and did my best to target bullying and bitchiness. By the time I was in Year 12 I was sticking up for both boys and girls who were in the same position I was at that age. If you are a target of bullying remember there is nothing wrong with going to a teacher if you are fearful. My advice, don't fight back. Prove you are better and stronger than to get sucked into that horrible and useless world.

My final words, there is no need to judge others on anything. You are at a pivotal point in your life where you create the person and adult you want to be. Focus on that and the rest will fall into place easily.

Tahyna Tozzi, model/actress

It's all about the BIG

Communication

Now that you've learned how to handle conflict, how to deflect a put-down and how to negotiate boundaries, it's time to polish your communication skills so you can be clearly understood and become a good listener.

There are not many girls who don't know how to talk, but how many girls are really good at listening? Over the past few years heaps of girls have asked me for advice about how to deal with a friend who purges all her problems and leaves no space for her friend to air her stuff. The common complaint is that it's really hard for teenage girls to create two-way streets in relationships. The fact is relationships need open lines of communication and they also need a lot of give and take. Being a good listener is just as important to friendship as being a good sharer.

You're about to learn how to really listen to what your friends are saying so you can reduce the chance of misunderstandings. And you're also going to learn how to decode what guys say, so you can cross the male-female communication divide. Finally, you're going to learn how to ace up your communication skills so you can speak in a way that honours both you and your friends.

"

I turned to my friends when it came to writing this, as they are the ones that contribute so much to my life.

I used to be impatient with my friends (actually with everyone) when I was growing up and never had the time to listen. I have realised that to be a good listener is one of the greatest qualities you can have. Being silent and having an opinion on a situation is far more satisfying for the friendship.

My friends are scattered across the globe, come from all walks and talks of life but we are all united by the same life values. We wake every day with passion in our eyes, a smile on our faces with the joy of life and everything that lies ahead. We believe in living in the present and not trying to pre-empt the future or hold on to anything that has happened in the past. One of the great teachings of Buddhism is if it won't affect you in 10 years, or if you won't remember it for that matter – let it go! I have one rule when it comes to friends and feuds – solve it there and then!

A quote by Tim McGraw that a friend of mine lives by is 'We all take different paths in life, but no matter where we go, we take a little of each other everywhere.'

The beautiful thing about friendship is that at the oddest times and in the most unexpected circumstances, a friend will say something to point you in the right direction through life and often have the ability to see things for what they really are. Friends know when to say things and when not to.

Cathy van der Meulen, businesswoman/
International Brand Manager, Supré

"

You've just listened to a friend for an hour while she spilled all her secrets. Now you feel tired and drained. Ever wondered why?

When to listen & when to talk

The reason you feel bad is that your friend has used you as a dumping ground for all her stress. Instead of having a two-way conversation where you shared in equal amounts, you allowed your friend to take advantage of you as a captive audience. She feels great and you feel terrible. But before you blame her for it you need to figure out why you allowed her to do that. Are you afraid of intimacy? Are you withholding information from your friend or are you allowing yourself to be a victim?

On the other side of the coin, if you recognise yourself as a big talker, you need to ask yourself if you're also a poor listener. Are you the one who gabs on while your friend sits in silence nodding away? Are you a chatterbox who leaves little space for others to share? And if so, why are you like that? Do your parents listen to you? Do you feel 'heard' in your relationships?

The answers to these questions are not easy, but it's important to look at your friendship dynamics and get the balance between sharing and listening right.

It's time to get conscious about how much you listen and how much you talk in your relationships. I'm not suggesting you set a clock and dole out equal amounts of time to listening and sharing, but I am suggesting you get clear about whether you're a good communicator or not (and if not, spruce it up with the following tips and techniques). Then become conscious about how much time in your relationships you take up with listening and sharing.

Miss-Understood or Miss Perfectly Clear.
Do this quiz to find out whether you are a good communicator.

1. When the teacher asks you to call out an answer do you:

   a) Blush horribly and just umm and ahh.

   b) You're ready with the answer and fire it back.

2. You're introduced to your boyfriend's parents for the first time. How do you act?

   a) I'm so excited to meet them I extend my hand to his dad and smile openly at his mum.

   b) I am so nervous I have sweaty palms and can hardly look them in the eyes.

3. You go to a fancy restaurant for dinner with friends and the waiter gives you the wrong meal. What do you do?

   a) I just eat what is put in front of me. I couldn't draw attention to myself by telling him he made a mistake.

   b) Call the waiter over pronto and ask him to fix the mistake.

4. You and your bestie are having an animated discussion about climate change. In front of the group she declares that the world will end in less than a decade (which you know is factually wrong). Do you:

   a) Correct her in a nice way right then and there.

   b) Say nothing because you don't want to embarrass her or yourself.

5. Someone you don't know well makes some snide remark about you as you pass them in the school corridor. Do you:

a) Just grin and bear it and pretend you didn't hear.

b) Turn around and say instantly, 'Did you say something? If you did I'd really like you to say it to my face.'

6. Which statement best describes your communication style?

a) Shy, introverted, nervous.

b) Upfront, extroverted, confident.

7. Your boss asks you to work an extra shift at work but it means you're going to miss your friend's party. Do you:

a) Agree to do it because you're scared that you'll lose your job if you rock the boat.

b) Apologise for not being able to help her out but tell her that unfortunately you can't do it.

8. It's public speaking day at school. You feel:

a) Exhilarated and excited. You like an opportunity to express your opinion and shine in public.

b) Like crawling under a rock. You'd rather die than stand up in front of the whole school and make them listen to boring old you.

1. a) 1   b) 3
2. a) 3   b) 1
3. a) 1   b) 3
4. a) 3   b) 1
5. a) 1   b) 3
6. a) 1   b) 3
7. a) 1   b) 3
8. a) 3   b) 1

24–12 Miss Confidence

You are a direct communicator. You are not afraid of standing up for yourself or others if you see an injustice. You're upfront, straightforward and open. People know where they stand with you and you're not likely to be bullied or pushed around. You are a good mediator, and you're probably called on to sort out misunderstandings in your group. You are good at seeing the big picture. You're a good talker, but sometimes you also need to be a good listener, so tune in to what other people are saying so that everyone feels heard and appreciated.

12-0 Shy Girl

You need a confidence injection Miss Shy Girl. While it's OK to be on the shy side, (which probably means you're more comfortable talking to small groups rather than large ones), it's not OK when you don't have enough confidence to stand up for your rights and needs. There are times when it's necessary to be in people's faces if you want something done or you need to be heard. You need practice at getting your own way and allowing yourself to be the centre of attention. It doesn't mean you're up yourself, it simply means you have the confidence to speak up, be heard and have your needs met. Time to trust that you're interesting and deserve to be heard!

12 effective communication tips

♥ To be a good communicator you also have to be a good listener. The way to do that is to put yourself in other people's shoes.

♥ Focus on what you want to achieve from your communication and aim to put action behind your words.

♥ Show that you can see the other person's side of the story so you build trust with them.

♥ Don't assume the other person is miles away from your point of view. Begin your conversations from a position of gentleness and calm. Don't look for trouble.

♥ Speak the truth with integrity.

♥ Try to begin with an open and positive statement such as: 'I know we can both get what we want out of this.' Don't put the other person down or start with negatives or put-downs.

♥ Have a message, be brief and listen carefully.

♥ Allow for silences. It's OK to think before you open your mouth.

♥ Make sure you say sorry if you interrupt. This will show you how often you're breaking the other person's concentration.

♥ Be personal without making it personal. Tell it how it is from your side without being defensive or making the other person feel that they are wrong.

♥ Got tummy butterflies? Take a deep breath and hold it for 5 seconds, then let it out for 5 seconds. Repeat until you feel calmer.

♥ Be compassionate. Cultivate an open heart and be soft and gentle with your friends.

Do you have a mobile phone?
Yes   91%
No   9%

How long do you talk on your
mobile phone to your friends?
5 minutes per day
10 minutes per day   64%
Half an hour per day   26%
More than one hour per day   22%
                                      18%

Do you use a chat room or website
(eg, myspace.com) to communicate
with your friends?
Yes
No   79%
                                      21%

How often do you text your friends?
Once a day   38%
Twice a day   22%
More than 5 times per day   20%
More than 10 times per day   20%

best friends 4eva!

Challenging negative thoughts so you can

communicate effectively

'The secret to having a good quality relationship with your friends (or with anyone, for that matter) is to communicate and think clearly,' explains Dr Tim Sharp from The Happiness Institute. 'It's important to remember that thoughts aren't always facts, they're ideas you have about a person or a situation.'

What you need to know is that when your thoughts are unhelpfully negative – Tim calls them ANTS or automatic negative thoughts – you'll struggle in relationships.
'The trick is to analyse your thoughts, question them, challenge them and ultimately come up with more helpful and more realistic thoughts,' says Tim.

...The good news is that negative thoughts can be changed! Although we all have unhelpful and negative thoughts from time to time, and we're not always very aware of them, it's empowering to know that by challenging or questioning these thoughts they can be changed – and that once that happens you'll feel happier and more in control and you'll also have much better quality relationships.

Are you friends with boys
(that are not your boyfriend)?
Yes   90%
No   10%

Who do you think makes
the better friend?
Girls   54%
Boys   46%

to challenge negative thoughts.

1. Be aware of what you are saying to yourself. Ask yourself:
    'What is going through my mind?' or
    'What is it about this situation that is upsetting me?'

2. Challenge your thoughts.
    (Remember, just because you think
    something doesn't mean it's true). Ask yourself:
    Is this thought helpful?
    Am I being realistic?

3. Consider the following strategies and ask
    yourself some of these questions:

Look for evidence
What's the evidence for and against my thought?
Am I focusing on the negatives and ignoring other information?
Am I jumping to conclusions without looking at all the facts?

Search for alternative explanations
Are there any other possible explanations?
Is there another way of looking at this?
How would someone else think if they were in this situation?
Am I being too inflexible in my thinking?

Put thoughts into perspective
Is it as bad as I am making out?
What is the worst that could happen?
How likely is it that the worst will happen?
Even if it did happen, would it really be that bad?
What could I do to get through it?

4. What is a more helpful thought?
    What can I say to myself that will help me remain calmer and
    help me achieve what I want to achieve in this situation?

OK, well my friends mean the world to me but so does my boyfriend. If my friends have something to say about someone in our group we sit down and talk about what is going on. Even if someone doesn't want to talk about it —we try and get them to talk because in our group we think it is important to talk about issues and things that are happening. Like the other week just before school ended, one of the girls said something about my boyfriend so we sat down and talked about it because she didn't even know him, but its good to talk about things — that's why I love my friends.' Kira, 15

The
secrets of happy relationships
with *boys*

How to read
the signs

One of the weird things we humans do with relationships is that we make assumptions about what other people think and feel. We find ourselves interpreting what they say through our own personal filters and while our emotional radars are right a lot of the time, we can also make mistakes and misinterpret people's meanings and actions too.

Relationships between boys and girls, and men and women, can send us crazy. We've all experienced times when we've wracked our brains trying to figure out what he, (or she) is trying to say to us. Who hasn't got a mixed message from a crush? During our teenage years, as we're learning how to make sense of people's signals and read between the lines, we are probably more prone than at any other time in our lives to interpret those signs and signals inappropriately. If you want to learn how to understand boys and what they're really saying to you, read on!

The first thing to understand is that the way WE think about things is important in the process of working out how we feel. There are times when our thoughts are negative (ANTs (see p 106), and when this happens we interpret and assume the communication from the other person is going to be negative too. To get clear, open and honest communication with people it's really important to recognise our own negative thoughts so we can learn how to change them.

Here are some common types of negative thoughts. (I asked Dr Tim from The Happiness Institute so you get the message about how we can misinterpret what boys are saying or doing. These answers can also apply to any situation where an automatic negative thought can prevent you from achieving a positive outcome.)

1) Over-generalisation

Means coming to a general conclusion based on a single event or one piece of evidence. If something bad happens once you expect it to happen again and again. Such thoughts often include the words 'always' and 'never'. For example,

He didn't want to go out with me. I'll always be lonely.

2) Selective filtering

Means concentrating on the negatives while ignoring the positives. So what you tend to do in this instance is ignore the important positive information about a situation. For example,

I know he said I looked great, but he also said he preferred it when I did my hair the way I used to — he really thought I looked terrible.

3) All or nothing thinking

Means thinking in black and white terms in that situations are either right or wrong, good or bad and that there are no definitions in between. A tendency to view things at the extremes with no middle ground. For example,

I really like him and he has so many things going for him but I really don't like the way he acts when he's with his mates so this relationship will never work.

4) Personalising

Means taking responsibility for something that's not your fault and thinking that what people say or do is some kind of reaction to you, or is in some way related to you. For example,

John's in a terrible mood. It must have been something I've done. It's obvious he doesn't like me, otherwise he would've been friendlier.

5) Catastrophising

Means always expecting something unbearable or intolerable to happen, that the worst possible scenario will become a reality. For example,

If I say no to him he'll break-up with me and I just couldn't cope with that – it would just be too terrible!

6) Emotional reasoning

Means mistaking feelings for facts. Negative things you feel about yourself are held to be true because they feel true. For example,

I feel ugly, therefore I must be ugly.

7) Mind reading

Means making assumptions about other people's thoughts, feelings and behaviours without checking the evidence first. For example,

John's talking to Molly so he must like her more than me... I knew he never really liked me.

Means anticipating an outcome and assuming your prediction is an established fact. These negative expectations can be self-fulfilling: predicting what we would do on the basis of past behaviour may prevent the possibility of change. For example,

I've always been like this; I'll never be able to change. It's not going to work out so there's not much point even trying. This relationship is sure to fail (before it even starts).

8) Fortune-telling error

Means using 'should', 'ought', or 'must' statements, which can set up unrealistic expectations of yourself and others. It involves operating by rigid rules and not allowing for flexibility. For example,

I shouldn't get angry. We shouldn't ever argue or disagree. People should be nice to me all the time.

9) Should statements

10) Magnification/Minimisation

Refers to a tendency to exaggerate the importance of negative information or experiences, while trivialising or reducing the significance of positive information or experiences. For example,

He noticed I spilled something on my shirt. I know he said he will go out with me again, but I bet he doesn't call. Supporting my friend when her mother died still doesn't make up for that time I got angry at her last year.

'I am popular with the guys at school, however I can't seem to fit in with most of the girls. I haven't done anything to them, but they just don't seem to include me in their conversations or parties, etc. When they do talk to me (very rare) they don't talk to me as they would with any other friend of theirs. It's like they don't feel comfortable with me around or something…? I feel the guys are more accepting and don't really judge me. The majority of the girls don't really accept newcomers and only stick to their little group of friends. Most of the guys that are my friends have fallen for me, but its kinda hard 'cause I really like this other guy and I don't like my guy friends as more than friends. Sometimes the chicks and other guys tease me 'cause I've got more guy friends than girlfriends. They're always like "Can't you choose one boyfriend. You can't have the lot, you know!" They can be really bitchy like that. It's kinda annoying. I wish everyone could just be friends with anyone 'cause it's like the chicks mainly judge people before they get to know them.' Meagan, 14

"Friendship is one of the great joys of life. Friends are like the family you choose to have around you, through good times and bad. My husband and I were friends before we became a couple and he is still my best friend. There is nothing better than a long rave with my beautiful mum on the telephone or a day spent sipping tea and talking with my dear girlfriends. When the world gets busier and busier you have to work at prioritising friendship time, particularly with two sons and a husband around me almost always (!). I crave and need my girly time with my friends regularly! I would drop anything for my friends – to be there for them and I know they would do the same for me. I am also very loyal. Like anything friendship goes through good and bad times, but at the end of the day your true friends will always love you and be there for you and is a great comfort in this busy world.

Katie Noonan, singer"

Some of the stuff that will show up on your path to good friendship karma

No matter how sophisticated our society becomes there are some issues that return to each generation and continue to challenge friendships.

Issues such as sexuality, the onset of puberty, money, what to do when a friend is depressed and what to do when friendship fades are perennial friendship questions. I've brought these issues up here because they're issues that need to be dealt with, and they're issues that I've been asked about many times. If you have a friend who is depressed or a friend who is hurting herself, the main thing you need to know is that you can't go it alone. Seek advice fast and don't try to fix any issue that is threatening a friend's wellbeing by yourself.

Many of the things I've brought up here will resolve themselves in time. But they can feel very big and scary when you're facing them! The best advice I can give you is ride the wave, take it in your stride and take a deep breath. My guess is that once your friendship has come through some of these challenges it will be stronger and happier than ever!

One of the biggest challenges to a friendship is that moment when your bestie, or several members of your group, begin a relationship with a boy. It's especially hard when you're at the stage where you're completely content contemplating the latest hottie on TV while she's fully ready to go all the way with her crush. The not-so-good news is that you can't wind back the clock, but the good news is that there are ways to help you and your friend get through this challenging phase.

★ Give her space to explore her new feelings and don't judge her.

★ If you don't like her crush the best strategy is to volunteer your thoughts about him only when asked – you may think you're protecting her from making a mistake by telling her he's a loser, but she'll just read it as jealousy. If he's 'bad' for her she'll find out in her own good time. It's your job to support her through the good and bad times.

★ Be OK, where you're at and accept yourself.

★ Get super-informed about unwanted pregnancies and sexually transmitted diseases – do it together so you share the wisdom.

★ Ask all about HER feelings.

★ If you feel safe, share your feelings with her and tell her you're a little worried she'll outgrow you. If she's a good friend she'll allay your fears.

★ Be interested in him – he might turn out to be your friend too!

★ Remember you can learn a lot through watching your friends – at times they'll make mistakes (and so will you) and at times they'll triumph. Listen, look and learn.

Boy stuff

I'm ready but
my bestie isn't

What's uppermost in your mind right now is that you'll grow apart because you're ready to go deeper with your crush and your friend is not at that stage. What you need to know is that it's OK. We all develop at different rates. There's a lot you can do to protect your relationship with your bestie while you're developing a more intimate relationship with a boy.

Here's how to stay friendship-smart during this tricky time:

✳ While it's important to have time with your crush, leave time for her too.

✳ Invite her with him (so they can get to know each other better) to some parties or group activities (don't take her on a date with you or she'll feel like the third wheel).

✳ Try not to be too intimate with him (like pashing for hours) in front of her. Just hold hands or give him a quick kiss or cuddle while you're with her.

✳ Share your feelings about him with her, but don't tell her everything – you don't want to embarrass or overload her with too much information.

✳ Maintain your interest in her life. If she's still interested in things you consider 'immature' just indulge her, she'll catch up in no time.

be sex smart

together

If you're ready to explore your sensual side and have some sort of sexual contact with a guy, here's what you need to know.

❤ About 60 per cent of Year 10 students and 75 per cent of Year 12 students have had some form of sexual contact.

❤ Approximately 26 per cent of Year 10 students have had sex

❤ About 47 per cent of Year 12 students have had sex.

❤ About 26 per cent of Year 10 students report mixing sex and alcohol.

❤ At least 20 per cent of Year 12 students report mixing sex and alcohol.

What these stats mean is that as you're reading this book the chances are that you've already had some experience with the opposite sex. It also means that you or your friends might have been drunk while you had sexual contact with a boy. This is kinda sad. Sex can be beautiful, romantic and a loving experience. If you're intoxicated, if you have little self-esteem and lack the confidence to set your boundaries with the opposite sex it can be rough, tragic, abusive and dumb.

If you want to enjoy sex and have fun with guys here are a few tips.

There's no such thing as being a dud kisser – it's all about the right time, the right person, the freedom to express yourself naturally and the safety to explore and experiment.

Don't have sex – even kiss – when you're seriously intoxicated

Try not to take being dissed or dumped too seriously. The right guy will love you for you and be just as desperate to hang out with you as you are with him.

It's vital that you decide how far you want to go. Oral sex or any other foreplay such as mutual masturbation, even tongue kissing should be reserved for a time you feel comfortable and ready to explore those sides of sex.

No matter what anyone tells you, oral sex is still sex and there are some risks such as herpes and other sexually transmitted diseases.

Condoms are not 100 per cent safe but they will give you reasonable protection you against many common STDs and give you protection against unwanted pregnancy. For more info about contraception check out Family Planning Australia's website *www.fpahealth.org.au* and go to the 'Sex Matters: Fact sheet' or call 1300 658 886.

You don't have to have sex just because all your friends are doing it. GirlForce flows when you have sex when you're ready.

Don't mix sex and drugs.

Without wanting to scare you or put you off sex, it can have serious consequences which are worth considering such as: unwanted pregnancy; sexually transmitted diseases such as herpes, warts, hepatitis B and C, chlamydia, syphilis, gonorrhoea and HIV.

No means NO. No is not negotiable. If you don't want to have sex with a boy make sure you negotiate your boundaries before you are in a vulnerable position. Alcohol and drugs can compromise the way you communicate your boundaries and make them harder for him to read.

Friends and money

By now you've probably noticed that some of your friends have loads of cash to burn while others seem to be skint all the time.

Money is not an issue that's often talked about between friends, but it's something that will challenge your relationships throughout your life. There's not a person on the planet that doesn't crave more money to spend. Whether you covet a mean guitar, a hot pair of heels, money to save for your first apartment, a trip to celebrate the end of school – whatever it is, money often figures in your plans for fun.

From an early age people start displaying their values around money. There's always one friend who wants to split the bill down to the last cent and another who loves to lavish gifts on her nearest and dearest.

Dos

Here are some basic rules when it comes to money and friendship.

☆ Negotiate an appropriate allowance with your parents.

☆ Get a casual job – if it doesn't put too much pressure on your studies.

☆ Save money – start good money habits early in life. There are some good websites such as www.understandingmoney.gov.au that can show you how to save your money with stuff like checking out mobile phones, budgeting, having a saving plan.

☆ Be generous when you can – and frugal when you can't.

☆ Going out with your friends doesn't have to cost the earth – think of fun things to do together that don't involve much ready cash – go to the beach, visit an art gallery, watch a DVD you've seen a million times and act out the scenes, make a scrapbook of your friendship, picnic in a park, give each other a facial, make a silly movie, compose a song, do a make-over on your friends.

Whatever your values are around money, it's important to be clear about how you like to behave with your precious dollars and let your friends know what your values are too.

Dont's

☆ Don't compare what you have to your friends – there will always be someone who has more than you, but at the same time there will be many who have less.

☆ Be careful when you lend money to friends - adding money issues to a friendship can have disastrous consequences.

☆ If you're very attached to your stuff don't lend your friends precious things that can't be replaced.

☆ Don't brag about what you have, be discrete about your money, your family's money and your possessions.

☆ Don't borrow money from friends without a strict plan of repayment that you can stick to.

☆ Don't allow your friends to pressure you into spending more than you feel comfortable with on clothes and entertainment. But do be open to spending a bit more when it means you'll miss out on important group activities.

Picture this: You're in your gym class looking down a row of bodies. You can see that Emma is long and leggy and has small boobs. Sally is curvy and has D cups (which she's had since Year 6), Jade is really athletic with a muscular body and B-cup breasts, and there's Caitlin who looks like a 10 year old. And then there's *YOU*.

Boobs, bras, periods and other girlie issues

Arrrgh. Sound familiar? We all develop at different rates and we all get physical gifts – and some things we're not so happy about – small boobs, hairy limbs, chunky thighs, zits, body odour, painful periods, ample hips. Most girls are prone to feeling uncomfortable about some part of their anatomy or the way they look. My *GirlForce* books are all about celebrating yourself just the way you are, so I won't go into how to bolster your self-esteem or how to love your body for the shape and size it is now, but what I will say is that a lot of pain comes from comparing ourselves with our friends.

Some girls will get big boobs while some girls will only ever develop little boobs. Some girls will always be curvy no matter how hard they try to slim down and some girls will struggle to put on an ounce of weight no matter how much they eat. We are all different and what we need to do as women is celebrate our differences. I hate hearing that girls have been teased because their bodies have not yet developed. (Unfortunately, I've heard this a lot and it makes me really sad.) It also makes me mourn for the state of our world when I hear girls are isolated because they're overweight or accused of being anorexic if they're naturally on the skinny side. It's time we stopped judging ourselves by a rigid set of rules that state what is attractive and what is not! When we stop feeling that we are unattractive we'll stop teasing and bullying others about the way they look too!

Let's make a pact to accept our shapes and sizes, our rates of development and our race and colour and love ourselves for who and what we are. Let's stop comparing ourselves to our friends and just enjoy being girls.

'Friendships are vital to growing up. Ever since you were a little kid you've had them. It didn't used to matter if they were guys or girls, white or black, fat or thin, 'ugly' or pretty, but now it does. We now judge people by their sex and their appearance. You can't just be friends with a boy. He has to be your boyfriend. You can't be friends with someone with a different skin colour to yours. You can't be friends with fat people. They let themselves get fat so they aren't allowed to have friends, worse, they don't deserve friends and fat people are automatically ugly. If you hang out with fat people you'll get fat too. You can't be friends with 'ugly' people. They look disgusting so you can't be seen with them. If you hang out with 'ugly' people you can't hang out with anyone else. If you are friends with 'ugly' people then you have sacrificed whatever popularity you had. Stereotypes! Our entire socail system revolves around them! Ditch the status quo and be friends with who you wanna be! Don't be another 'mean girl'! If you ignore someone because of their apperance, you could miss out on the greatest friendship of your life!' Jess, 13

Friends & depression

There are times
in life
when we all
get a bit blue.

A poor exam result, being dissed by a boy or teased by your friends are all things that can make you feel low. Depression is one of the biggest health crises of our times. It costs the health system millions and millions of dollars and it costs families more in terms of the heartbreak and sadness it causes. The good news is that depression can be treated, but it needs to be treated by professionals, doctors and psychologists.

I asked Professor David Bennett, Head, NSW Centre for the Advancement of Adolescent Health, The Children's Hospital at Westmead to explain the difference between sadness and depression and here's what he said.

Youth depression has tripled in the last thirty years. About 30 per cent of young people will have experienced a mental health problem by the age of 18. Unfortunately, only about 50 per cent of depression sufferers are recognised and adequately treated. This is very worrying because depressed teenagers often become depressed adults.

What can be really challenging for teenagers is to determine whether they are sad, because something has happened to them or is happening (such as bullying), or whether they are actually depressed? The best place to start is with a definition. Essentially depression can be diagnosed when sadness lasts longer than two weeks and is associated with physical symptoms such as weight loss or gain, appetite and sleep changes, sudden changes in school performance and sudden changes in relationships.

As doctors we usually ask the following questions to determine whether someone is depressed.

- How long have you been feeling sad?
- How has your schoolwork been going?
- What are you interested in?
- How do you find your friendships with other people?
- How is your appetite? Have you lost or gained weight recently?
- How are you sleeping?
- Is there something that is making you sad? If it stopped would you feel completely better? Would it fix everything?

The signs of of depression include:

- Depressed or irritable moods lasting most of the day, nearly every day. A sense of hopelessness, tearfulness, anxiety, aches and pains, persistent anger.

- A decreased interest or pleasure in all or almost all activities.

- A significant change in weight.

- Sleeping problems – commonly a lack of sleep or oversleeping: sometimes waking early and experiencing difficulty returning to sleep.

- Physical agitation: an inability to sit still, pacing, and hand wringing.

- Fatigue or loss of energy.

- Feelings of worthlessness or excessive guilt.

- A decreased ability to think or concentrate.

- Thoughts of death.

Young people with depression may also experience the following.

- Irritability.

- Failure to make expected weight gains.

- Diminished school performance.

- Unexplained boredom.

- Anxiety.

- Social withdrawal and isolation.

- Physical complaints without physical cause.

- Depression tends to run in families.
- It is in part due to a chemical imbalance in the brain.
- It may be associated with personal tragedies or significant life changes.
- It is more likely in people who are sensitive, emotional, perfectionists and dependent.
- It may be a learned response for people who have repeated losses, stress or who experience 'depressed thinking'.

Professor David Bennet recommends seeking help if you or your friends experience any of the symptoms.

The big question is why is adolescent depression increasing? Many theories have been put forward: social change, world turmoil, substance abuse, hopelessness, exposure to bullying and violence and lack of spirituality leading to inner emptiness and turmoil.

Given that the world can be a difficult place,

it's not surprising that many young people

have negative inner beliefs and struggle

to find meaning in life.

What's important to understand though, is that depression is very different to normal unhappiness. It is prolonged intense sadness that interferes with our ability to function. It's a medical condition that needs medical help and intervention. The good news is that there are solutions. On the positive side too, depression is very treatable. Certain 'talking therapies' such as Cognitive Behavioural Therapy, which challenges negative thinking, and certain medications, have been shown to help depression.

✳ Only a doctor is qualified to make these assessments.

The trick is for teenagers to get help! Teenagers are often worried they will be labelled as weird and tend to put off seeking appropriate care. If you are depressed, or one of your friends is depressed, the first thing you must do is seek out a trusted adult or medical professional. (Look through the contact details for help lines at the back of this book). The next thing you need to do is give yourself or your friend a break – don't judge yourself or others harshly if you or your friend are depressed. What you need to do is take positive action to get help and get it fast!

My friend is talking about suicide

According to Professor David Bennett, mentioning suicide does not necessarily mean a person is going to kill themselves, but it's worth taking any threat seriously and reporting it immediately to an adult, school counsellor or health professional you trust. If you're worried, chances are that your instincts are right. Your friend may not be suicidal, but they may be depressed. Whatever you do, don't brush it off or play it down. Don't be judgemental, don't allow yourself to be sworn to secrecy and try not to get into a panic. It's important that they are not left alone. If you're concerned about a friend's behaviour let them know you are not capable of helping them on your own, you need help to deal with their crisis. By all means tell them you are there for them and you love them and care for them, but be firm about your need to get professional help. It's important to note that more than 90 per cent of depressed and suicidal young people confide in a friend before they take their life.

She's hurting herself

Suddenly you notice that your bestie has dropped a lot of weight. Or she's got cut marks on her inner thighs that she's hidden from her parents. Or she's binge drinking at parties to the point where she passes out and can't remember a thing the next day. Sound familiar? Many girls and guys your age report these sorts of things going on with their friends. The challenge is what to do about it?

The first thing you need to do is gently ask your friend what's going on. The chances are they'll deny there's anything wrong. If she or he admits they have a problem, suggest they see their family doctor, speak to their parents and seek help from one of the many organisations that help with teen depression, drug addiction or other self-harming behaviours (maybe write down the contact details for Beyond Blue, Kids Help Line or the Butterfly Foundation and have it ready to hand them when you have the conversation?) What you need to know is that any behaviour that risks your health, or your friend's health, happiness and wellbeing, is not OK and needs professional help – FAST.

When to tell

One of the biggest challenges to a friendship is when one (or both) parties begins to do risky things such as taking drugs, drinking alcohol, following excessive diets or purging and self-harming. Even though you may think you are being her or his friend by listening, the truth is that listening is not enough. You are not a health professional and you cannot treat their problems. Aside from the fact that it's an excessive burden for you as the friend to bear, you will not be helping your friend by keeping your mouth shut. When you notice your friends are taking undue risks with their health and wellbeing it's very important for you to report it, either to your school counsellor, a doctor or your parents. You can do some research for yourself by calling the Kid's Help Line or contacting one of the agencies outlined at the back of this book.

There are many reasons a friendship fades and at times, eventually ends. Sometimes it's simply a matter of outgrowing each other and discovering that you've gone in different directions. Sometimes it's because one of you gets a boyfriend and wants to spend all available time with him. And sometimes it's because your friends are acting in ways that cross your boundaries.

Whatever the reason for your break-up, it's often traumatic and sad.

Like all things to do with relationships there are always two sides of the story – the one who is leaving and the one who is left (unless you mutually decide to end a relationship, usually one party ends up cutting the ties). Whether you are the person who wants to let the friendship go, or the person who is still hanging in there and coming to terms with the loss, the most important thing is to do is communicate how you're feeling openly, honestly and most importantly, compassionately.

What to do when
friendship fades

If you're the one who wants to leave a friendship what you need to know is that the worst thing you can do is just end it – you'll feel guilty and the friend will feel wounded, abandoned, confused, rejected and abused. Walking away from a relationship or ending it very abruptly leaves no room for closure, which is especially helpful to the person who is left.

A letter can often be the best way to gently end a friendship or let a friend know that you're sorry things are going off the rails. If you're ending a friendship don't text it, that's brutal, and I wouldn't suggest emailing either, as it's too spontaneous and you can say things you don't mean. When you sit down and handwrite all the reasons why you want to end a relationship or save it, you will have time to consider your response and you'll formalise your thoughts.

When a friendship is ending it can be very easy to make the other person wrong – it stops you feeling guilty and you avoid taking responsibility for your part in the break-up. Whether you're the dumper or the dumpee, you need to own up to the reasons why the relationship is breaking down and own your part of the responsibility.

If you want to end a relationship responsibility I suggest that you communicate to the other person that you think it's time to part ways (there's nothing worse for you or the other party when you're hanging on to a broken relationship – it becomes torturous).

I've been asked many times how to end a friendship compassionately and effectively and here's my script.

'Hi. Do you have time to talk? By now you're probably aware that our friendship has been a bit rocky. It's become clear to me that we've gone in different directions. I'm sorry that this has been painful for both of us but I think we both have very different expectations of this relationship'. I've been feeling very sad about if for a while and I've wracked my brains trying to find a solution to the problems in our relationship. Unfortunately I haven't been able to find a way through this and I want to say that I think we either need a break from one other, or we may need to end our relationship.

It can be hard to say out loud what you feel in such a circumstance, but it's a clear, clean, honest and honourable way to end a relationship. Chances are that you've hinted at wanting to let go for some time (not returned calls, been unavailable, you may have even given her the cold shoulder) and yet, she's clung to the relationship. By communicating your needs you've let her know, in a clear way, that you can't be a part of the friendship any longer, but you've also done it in a compassionate way.

If you're the one who's been left my advice is to try to let it go and move on. I won't diminish how painful this can be, but relationships break down all through your life and it's something that you need to chalk up to experience. Cry it out, talk it out, write about it in a journal – whatever you need to do to heal and get over the break-up do it! Try not to hold onto any resentments and try not to act out your upset by turning others against the friend who you broke up with – the best thing to do is move on and put your self-esteem in order. Remember you are loveable, valuable and unique, eventually you'll find a friend who knows that about you.

'My friends all turned against me and kicked me out of the group that I had started. It turned out that it was the best thing for me! Finally I had the confidence and the chance to meet new people and explore new friendships. I found out how many true friends I have, and all the people that care for me. As for those other girls... I don't need people who are going to bitch about me behind my back and hurt me... I'm the happiest I've ever been, so I guess I better say thank you to those bitches... 'cause when life hands me lemons, I make lemonade, baby!' Sarah, 15

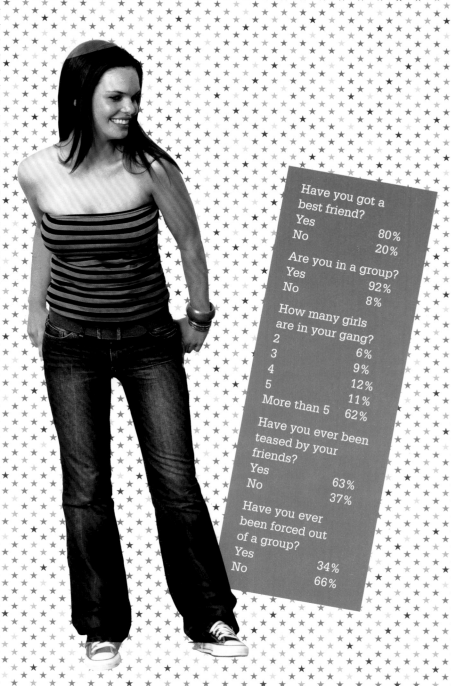

Have you got a
best friend?
Yes
No   80%
                  20%

Are you in a group?
Yes
No   92%
                  8%

How many girls
are in your gang?
2
3   6%
4   9%
5   12%
                  11%
More than 5   62%

Have you ever been
teased by your
friends?
Yes
No   63%
                  37%

Have you ever
been forced out
of a group?
Yes
No   34%
                  66%

What we discovered in the Friendship Survey we did with *Girlfriend* magazine was that 24 per cent of girls said they felt lonely and 34 per cent said their friends had forced them out of a group.

These statistics are very sad indeed.

The fact that SO many girls feel isolated, afraid, lonely and alone is a sad indictment on our society today. But the good news is there's a lot you can do about it. If you've been pushed out of your posse, dissed by your bestie or if you're lonely because you don't have many or any friends, you'll be comforted to know that with some relationship smarts, you can turn this around.

I'm alone

1

The first thing you need to do if you've been dumped by a friend or pushed out of your group is dust yourself off. It's a horrible, lonely feeling to be left alone, and it's scary not knowing who you'll sit with at school, but this feeling won't last. Don't catastrophise the situation. It's bad, but it's not the end of the world, you haven't lost a limb and you are not completely alone – most people have families and someone they can trust. Focus on the positives. Think about the people you DO have in your life and let the upset go.

If you're really devastated, and are feeling depressed, find someone professional to talk to, get some counselling and advice.

2

Cultivate new friends – join a sporting club, go to a yoga class or a dance class. Get really passionate about a charity and raise money for people less fortunate than you – get out there and socialise.

3

4

Ace up your grooming. Nothing says, 'I feel great about myself' than shiny locks, polished nails and great makeup. Get a makeover or reward yourself with a home facial or manicure (check out my book *Shine* for great tips and techniques for giving your image a super-boost).

Don't be afraid to talk to new people at school. Most girls know how it feels to be dissed and eventually you'll find a sympathetic group who will accept and love you for you. Try an approach such as, 'Hi. Would you believe it, I've made the biggest mistake of my life. I though XX was my friend. How wrong could I be? Would you mind if I sit with you for lunch?

5

6

Join an on-line forum with like-minded girls. Every week I've run the GirlForce Forum with girls all over Australia who have similar issues to you. The regular girls on the Forum have made friendships all around Australia. *www.girlforce.com.au*

7

'Don't worry, be happy' – be happy with yourself. Nothing acts as a magnet for relationships more than a person who is happy with themselves.

8

If you're very sad about what's happened to you write her (or them) a letter telling them that they hurt you and letting them know you're moving on. If you clear the air you'll feel less victimised – but be careful you don't write a vicious or vengeful letter. That will create more karma when what you're really trying to achieve is a clear and peaceful end to a conflict.

9

Let go – no matter what's happened to you, it's important to let go of your upset and move on.

10

If you have never had a friend it's possible you have some issues that need professional help. There may be something from your childhood that's preventing you from forming intimate ties with people or you may have very low self-esteem, which is also holding you back. Don't be afraid to admit that you have a problem and seek professional advice from a counsellor.

Could you describe yourself as lonely?
Yes   24%
No   76%

Forgive & forget

'The weak can never forgive. Forgiveness is the attribute of the strong.'

Mahatma Gandhi (1869 – 1948), political and spiritual leader of India

'Life is an adventure in forgiveness.'

Norman Cousins (1915 – 1990), journalist and world peace advocate

'Forgiveness is almost a selfish act because of its immense benefits to the one who forgives.'

Lawana Blackwell, author

Forgiveness is such a grand, yet complex emotion that I thought I'd start with some quotes on forgiveness.

'There is no revenge so complete as forgiveness.'

Josh Billings (1818 – 1885), 19th century humourist

Forgiveness is ultimately an act of self-love.

To hold onto anger, or to wish for revenge, is a toxin that eventually poisons the heart. To truly forgive is to let go of the past and live in the present. You don't forgive so you can be right. You forgive because it's the right thing to do. Holding on to hurt and anger hurts you – not the other person. It's an understatement to say it's hard to forgive! War, death, destruction and revenge have been the result of people not forgiving others for the wounds they've inflicted. But without forgiveness there is no peace, happiness, love or contentment.

A lack of forgiveness reveals a lack of trust in life's processes and ultimately a lack of self-love. If you deeply love yourself you will let go of your hurts. It can take time to forgive someone, but if you maintain an intention in your heart to let go and forgive, eventually it will happen.

There's not a person alive who has not suffered due to someone's carelessness, cruelty or maliciousness. All of us are wounded somehow, someway by someone. The challenge we all face is to find a place in our hearts to forgive, even the cruellest cuts, because what we're left with if we do not forgive is a wasteland of sorrow.

Let go and let your heart fill with love so you can forgive and ultimately forget.

'Holding on to anger, resentment and hurt only gives you tense muscles, a headache and a sore jaw from clenching your teeth. Forgiveness gives you back the laughter and lightness in your life.'

Joan Lunden (from *Healthy Living* magazine), American broadcaster

Friendship – It's a beautiful thing

Let's celebrate!

Treasure
what you have

I consider myself very lucky because I still have friends I met in high school. Those girls know me in ways that no-one who I've met since could imagine. We have been through so much together, hysterical laughter and bitter tears and all the highs and lows of life. What I've discovered is that some friendships are for life and some friendships are for a moment.

What I've also discovered is that it's not the length of time you've been friends but the quality of your relationships that matters. You can experience really intense feelings about someone you've only just met, and at times your oldest friends can let you down. The best relationships are built on trust, mutual values, compassion, acceptance, respect, kindness and honesty. And perhaps what gets you through it all is humour – having a good laugh together can get you through the toughest tests of your relationship. Cherish your friends and treasure what you have. Treasuring your friends is about taking the time to give thanks for what you have, and it's this sense of gratitude that will fill your heart with love and reaffirm for you how lucky you are to love those people you call your friends.

'I have a really, really great friend. We are so alike it is almost as though we are twins. I love her so much and I can't imagine life without her. I don't have many problems to talk to her about but if I did I know she would always be there. We have so much fun together! I know that if a boy was getting in the way of our friendship the boy would be out straightaway. I love her with all my heart and I know she loves me too. I thank God every day that I have been given such a great friend and that I have met my soul mate. Our love is stronger than any love I have ever seen'. Frances, 14

"

'I'm not a girlie girl and I've never been one of those people who liked to hang with a big group and sit around gossiping. I don't like to play games and I tell it how it is. I found that when I was at high school that didn't always sit well with a lot of girls. I had friends at school but no-one special. I waited 22 years to meet my best friend, Simone, but when finally met her everything changed. In Simone I found a friend I could really trust. Trust is a big thing for me and without it you can't have a really deep friendship. I've always been very private, but Simone made it safe for me to share myself with her. We celebrate each other's successes and we support each other through the tough times. She never puts me down and when she wants to be honest with me she tells me what she thinks with compassion. There's such a huge pressure to have heaps of girlfriends and I never did. I used to wonder whether I was boring! Meeting Simone taught me that it was worth waiting for that one amazing friend and I'm so grateful for that. It's OK to have lots of friends, but it's also OK to have one special friend. Simone helped me feel complete. We completely accept each other. When I think of her I always smile.' Ada Nicodemou, actress

"

No friendship is perfect because nobody is perfect.

You're not perfect, and neither are your friends. But not being perfect is no reason not to make and hold onto friends. Our friends may have habits that irritate us, quirks we don't understand and beliefs that we think are crazy, but it's those differences that make our friends interesting and our friendships fascinating.

If you focus on the things you don't like you'll end up letting go of a lot of friends. One of the most important things to learn about friendship is that we need to cultivate a level of acceptance about our friends. Learning to be tolerant of people's flaws and foibles will also give you much more space to accept yourself. It's vital to understand that hoping a friend will change is like wishing you can fly – it's not going to happen. If you want to change a relationship, what you need to do is change yourself – by altering your expectations and your approach to your friends.

When you allow a loving space in your heart you'll increase your level of acceptance of others. And letting go of your expectations about how your friends should look, think and behave will give you the wisdom to enjoy them for who they are. Let go of your judgements and practise being tolerant and accepting your friends for their weaknesses as well as their strengths.

> I came from a small country town and grew up in a close community where I had a great group of friends. That said, everyone got their turn with being bullied. Sometimes I was excluded and sometimes we excluded other girls. I regret that. What I've learned is that you need to treasure your friends and treat them with respect and kindness. No-one's perfect.
>
> Those friends you make early in life can be friends for life. I have a friend who I met when we were both in Grade 3. I had big ponytails and a cool watch and she thought that stuff was kinda great so we became friends. Later, she went to Adelaide and I went to Melbourne but we've stayed in touch and been there for each other through all the highs and lows.
>
> What you need from a friend is supportno matter what. To know they won't judge you or make you feel bad about yourself. A good friend is someone who allows you to make mistakes and loves you for your strengths and your weaknesses. They may pull you up at times but they do that with kindness. You don't need a million friends; you just need one friend who really knows you. That's a real friend.
>
> Myf Warhurst, television and radio personality

Acceptance

Be yourself

With peer pressure and the in-your-face-style of the media it's all too easy to loose track of who we are and what we value. We can get so tied up in what our friends expect of us that we forget to be ourselves and value our own identity. A successful friendship is not one where you loose yourself in the other. A successful friendship is one that values both parties equally for their differences as well as their shared traits and ideas.

I've been asked many times, 'How can I make myself more attractive to X or Y?' and the answer is simple. Be yourself! Don't try to change yourself to make yourself more palatable to someone else, accept yourself for who you are and value what you have. When you love and accept yourself, others will too.

'I've learnt a lot about friendship this year, which is ironic seeing as this is the year I've been away from my friends for almost seven months. Working in the film industry as a teenager and being on film sets, filming and networking can get really tiring. You're constantly trying to please people and do a good job. I remember the first time I spoke to my friend on Skype was after I had been away for five months. The moment I heard that familiar voice I was overcome with a feeling of freedom. It was like I immediately dropped the guard I had up for so long. It was the best feeling. I felt the most relaxed and the most myself I had been in months.

I'm so grateful to have those people in my life because I know I don't have to try to be anyone when I'm talking to them. I don't have to hide any aspect of my personality because who they like is me and all my flaws and weirdness. They give me the chance to take a deep breath out and let go.'

Mia Wasikowska, actress

Do your friends make you feel good about yourself?

Yes	87%
No	13%

How much time do you spend thinking about your friends?

Less than 1 hour a day	19%
More than 1 hour	41%
A lot of hours in the day	40%

HAVE FUN

Making relationships work can be really tough at times.

Navigating the 'rules' of a group or the demands of a bestie can leave us tired and drained. At these times it's especially important to remember to have fun. This is where being a girl comes into its own. Allow yourself to be silly, stress-down not out, chill out together and take a load off. Remember you're a teenager and get into the groove of being a kid not an adult, because those responsibilities will hit you all too soon.

Get your girls together, have a party and kick up your heels.

Love the life you lead

♥ Give each other flowers.

♥ Paint each other's nails.

♥ Bake a cake together.

♥ Go for a walk together.

♥ Go shopping.

♥ Dress up in each other's clothes.

♥ Start a charity together.

♥ Plant a tree.

♥ Surprise each other.

♥ Send each other cool quotes.

♥ Write an affirmation for her/him.

♥ Send your friends a card of appreciation.

♥ Give each other chocolate – so you are reminded of the sweetness of life.

♥ Pamper one another with a massage.

♥ Watch a daggy movie and laugh out loud together.

'I was a bit of a nomad growing up. During my school years my dad's work took us from Perth to Bangkok to Queensland. Then at the age of nineteen I decided to pack up my bags and drive to Sydney. It wasn't a move I thought through very well. In fact it was a decision driven by gut instinct more than anything else. But that same feeling has served me well since. My dad always said you have to let life take its course.

And so my course continues in Sydney seven years on, but it's only recently I've really felt settled. So what makes a place feel like home? There are many reasons, but only one that holds them all together. Friends are that foundation. They give meaning to your experiences – the most seemingly mundane of which can bring so much laughter simply because you're with that person.

True girlfriends are there for you no matter what the situation. They know you inside out and respect and care for you implicitly. They offer advice honestly but without judgement. I am very fortunate to have developed some beautiful friendships since moving to Sydney. But it takes time to find people you really connect with and they are few and far between. The fact it's taken so long for me to really feel at home here is testament to that.

For two years I shared a house with three gorgeous girls. We were all from Queensland and became a surrogate family to each other – a home away from home. Two of those girls have since moved overseas, but Melissa lives just around the corner from me now and we look after each other like family. It may seem like a cliché but friends are the family you choose. A tried and tested adage. A bit like a good friend really.'

Sara Groen, news presenter

Love you first

Sounds kind of corny but the best way to be a best friend is to love yourself first. It's not about being up yourself or being arrogant, it's about cultivating a strong sense of self-esteem and self-love so that you can love others freely. Hoping that a friend will complete you, fill up your empty soul or lift you up on a daily basis is not only too much to expect from another person, it also leaves you in a false state where you're craving love from all the wrong places – the truth is you have to fill in the gaps yourself. Loving you first is not easy. If we knew how to do that we'd all be enlightened.

The point is not to get it perfect, but to be conscious of the holes in our hearts and try, really try, to love ourselves as we are.

Practise this daily affirmation and feel your self-love grow inside you:

I love myself exactly as I am.

I experience love like a flowing river inside myself.

I know that people love me and I am free to love in return.

Everything in my world is as it should be.

CELEBRATE

WOW you've made it!

You've learned heaps of great stuff about how to handle the hard stuff, how to mean what you say and say what you mean and finally how to enjoy and treasure what you have. Wherever you were in the friendship stakes when you started reading this book, you should be feeling really good about your prospects for more and better friendships now that you have a grip on these cool tips and techniques.

Having friends is one of life's most beautiful gifts. If you have one person who you love and one person who loves you, you're blessed. Congratulate yourself for reading this book and being willing to work on your relationships! I want you to know that just the act of reading *Friends*, is making a contribution to your world – because anything you do to improve yourself and improve the lives of others brings us all just a little bit closer to a place of peace and harmony.

One thing I know now about friendships is that the best ones are about mutual love and respect. I also know that when I love and respect myself, my relationships improve. Don't be afraid to make your relationships better by working on them – you'll be rewarded if you have the courage to examine yourself and your relationships.

And one last word…Please do what you can to stamp out 'mean girl' behaviour, bullying and bitchiness, every little bit counts.

Love

Nikki

When a day feels like a tumbling spiral, and you're sinking into the middle of darkness, a hand reaches in, two hands, three hands. They pull at the light inside of you and make sure you never forget how beautiful you really are. Each person that takes your hands whistles a different tune. Sometimes their tune doesn't match your walk, these hands you let go. Sometimes their tune is the symphony of your step and these hands you hold for a lifetime. Most friends you have make small incisions into your life, they teach you something about who you are or who you could be. One moment you are the two closest souls in the world, the next a distant memory. But for those moments you are in tune with each other, you are there for each other, and you touch each other's lives in a way that is unforgettable. Friends are the hands that you hold throughout life. Sometimes you let go, but you never forget how it feels to be together as one.

Claire Clarke, singer/songwriter

Credits

I dedicate this book to all my friends.

My deepest thanks to Dr David Bennett, you're a living legend and a total inspiration. Thanks also go to Dr Tim Sharp, the guru of happiness, I am so grateful for your time, energy and integrity.

To all the girls who wrote from their hearts about friendship, I send you all my thanks. You made me laugh and cry. I wish I had room for all of your words. You are amazing.

Without the support of my loving and generous publishers, Belinda Bolliger and Jody Lee, GirlForce would never have seen the light of day. I thank you for your hard work and belief in me and my projects.

This book has come alive with the voices of brilliant, talented, powerful and generous women. From the bottom of my heart I thank Bridie Carter, Ada Nicodemou, Claire Clarke, Mia Wasikowska, Myf Warhurst, Noni Hazlehurst, Sanica Robinson, Sara Groen, Tara Rushton, Tahyna Tozzi, Pia Miranda, Katie Noonan and Cathy van der Meulen.

Your contributions made this book sing.

My thanks to Steven Chee and Prue Ruscoe, your photographs live on in this book and are still making a difference to girls' lives.

To all the agents who worked tirelessly behind the scenes to lasso their celebs, I thank you very much.

This book was made possible by the hard work of an incredible team of people and the contributions of thousands of Aussie girls, including some famous girls and women and some talented and generous professionals.

GirlForce wouldn't be GirlForce without the fresh faces of: Yasmin Suteja, Beata Khaidurova, Alia Pretzil, Lauren Sedger, Martina Pasqualino, Kat Bradley. Thank you forever girls!

To the team at *Girlfriend* magazine, you are such a great bunch of girls. I thank you so much for your enduring support and friendship.

Über-stylist Nadene Duncan, the publisher and I would like to thank the following organisations for their generous contribution of time, energy, clothes, props, accessories and shoes for this book: Target, Zimmerman, One Teaspoon, Ali, Blessed Of The Meek, Mermaid Sister, Splendid, Converse, Sunnygirl, Roxy, Peace Angel from Tree of Life, Diva, Equip accessories, Havianna, Pepe, Wrangler jeans, Dinosaur Designs, Mooks, Ella Moss, Mijo, Keds, Alibi, Milk and Honey, Mavi, Bonds, Jiiva, French Kitty, Tigerlily, La Senza, Esprit, Gorman, AM sunglasses, Moontide, Marcs.

Thank you to my family for surviving yet another book! I love you Rowan and Liberty.

Designer Nerida Orsatti has done a brilliant job. This book is beautiful and fascinating because you're a true talent. Thank you for making the process a breeze.

Thank you to all the models who appear in GirlForce books: Natalie Jayne Roser, Jessica McColl, Katie Dunkley, Charlotte Barge, Autumn Armstrong, Mikki Tracton, Ortenzia Borreggine, Elizabeth Green, Sarah Ash, Chris Mathews, William Horbacz, Eunice Ward, Emma Adams, Kieta Van Ewyk, Patric Rodrigues Fernandes and Hillary Andersen.

Friendship Resources

Australian Government Youth Site
www.thesource.gov.au

A gateway to youth information, programmes, services, resources and entertainment for young people between the ages of 12 and 25.

Beyond Blue National Depression Initiative
www.beyondblue.org.au

A great site with great information on identifying and dealing with depression.

Centre for Adolescent Health
(03) 9345 5890
www.rch.unimelb.edu.au/cah/index.cfm

A practical site on any issues to do with adolescent health and points of contact within the medical system.

Drug and Alcohol Council of Australia
www.adca.org.au

A site with real and practical information on drugs and alcohol use and abuse.

Get To Know Your Daughter
Parents Advice
www.gettoknowyourdaughter.com.au

A fab site that you can get your parents to look at to help them understand some of the issues that are particularly important to teenage girls.

GirlForce
www.girlforce.com.au

Get the complete lowdown on GirlForce and Girl Power.

Girlfriend magazine
www.girlfriend.com.au

The official magazine website.

The Happiness Institute
www.thehappinessinstitute.com

Dr Tim Sharp's site that gives all the information you need on getting and staying happy.

Lifeline   1300 13 11 14
www.lifeline.org.au

A site for when you need someone independent to talk to if you are feeling lonely, isolated or anxious about things in your life.

Kids Help Line   1800 551 800
www.kidshelp.com.au

A great source of information to help you deal with whatever life throws at you, providing good contacts for any type of help you want.